FARM-FRESH JOY *for* KITCHEN & TABLE

Seasons
TO TASTE

JONATHAN BARDZIK

STORY FARM

WINTER PARK • MIAMI • SANTA BARBARA

Seasons TO TASTE

The following photographers' work shares my food and story beautifully:
    Matt Hocking
    Martha FitzSimon :: marthafitzsimon.com
    Jenny Lehman :: jennylehman.com
    Megan Peper, MC Photography
    Garry Grueber, Cultivaris
    Front cover photo by Jenny Lehman

Book Design: Peter Gloege

ISBN 978-0-9905205-9-7

Library of Congress Cataloging-in-Publication Data
Bardzik, Jonathan
        Seasons To Taste : Farm-fresh joy for kitchen & table / Jonathan Bardzik
p. cm.

Published in Collaboration with Story Farm
Printed in China

Follow Jonathan Bardzik:
www.JonathanBardzik.com   ☐ (search) Jonathan Bardzik   ☐ @JonathanBardzik

TO EVERYONE WHO INSPIRES ME TO FIND
JOY IN THE KITCHEN.
YOU MADE THIS BOOK POSSIBLE.

ESPECIALLY MOM & DAD, KATIE & ALEC,
& MY HUSBAND JASON—OH, AND THE BEETS,
LOTS & LOTS OF BEETS.

winter

spring

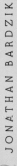

summer

fall

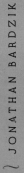

I WANT YOU TO FEEL JOY. Real joy.

Not the fleeting, easily replaced, brightly-wrapped pleasure of selfies and the flavorless strawberries that fill grocery stores in February, but the true joy of gathering with the people who make your life matter for dinners around the kitchen table. The joy of summer's sweetest peaches, available for only a few weeks. The ones that are so ripe, they are gently bruised before the bushel baskets leave the field.

Joy, true joy, isn't fleeting, it is scarce. And through that scarcity, it is precious. It's my brother's 7th birthday party, celebrated on a heavy August night, under our large covered porch. We bite the season's last truly sweet corn off the cob, kernels catching between our teeth. Juice runs down wrists and over chins from thick slabs of sugary watermelon. Aunts, uncles, grandmothers and cousins, brothers and sisters, gather together, easy and familiar, in the kitchen, at the grill, and around the table. Yesterday's freshly-cut grass still sticks to our bare feet, picked up on a dew-soaked morning walk out

to the vegetable garden, where we harvested the green beans, tomatoes and peppers that fill the table.

This moment will never happen again. These people, some now gone, will never gather as the same group. Next summer will be wetter or drier, hotter or cooler. We'll plant new varieties in our gardens and find a change of crops at the farm market. And this next summer, unique and scarce, like every other summer of our lives, will be precious and filled with joy.

The other seasons will be, too. A harvest of more turnips and fewer pumpkins will change Thanksgiving dinner. In a few years, we'll forget the high piles of snow, but remember the gift of unexpected pancake breakfasts on mornings of weather-bestowed leisure. Spring will return and we'll watch carefully as each plant emerges from the ground. We'll celebrate subtleties of color, form and flavor that would be lost amidst the approaching riot of summer's bright bounty.

As you read this book, as you cook the recipes, may each story and each meal be shaped by the people gathered at your table—both family and friends —and by the community of farmers and purveyors who connect you to food at its best, fresh and seasonal. Let this year's bounties shape each meal in a way that will never return, one that that will be truly precious. And then, next year, may you experience it—new, fresh, and different— all over again.

Jonathan

winter

HARD FOUGHT GLORY. When I was twelve, we had a particularly good spring thaw. Snow melting from the acres of hills up behind our house filled the streambed that runs the edge of our property. By the time it reached the culvert, which ran under the bridge out to the pasture, it was rushing violently—white, icy spray pouring through as it continued on its way.

To a young boy, this looked like the set of an action movie, something Harrison Ford would brave to reach a shining treasure. I just had to go in.

My parents were the one big obstacle. See, it was early March, there was still snow on the ground and the water was barely above freezing. Therefore, this seemed like a terrible idea to everyone but me. Yet, somehow I convinced them. My father walked me out to the bridge, wrapped up in layer upon layer of clothing, while Mom ran a hot bath upstairs.

And?

It was awesome! I don't think I spent more than thirty seconds in the water, but I stepped out a hero, having conquered villains, braved great struggles and saved the world. Five minutes later I sat, shivering, in the bathtub watching my bright pink legs regain their normal color while Mom's chicken soup waited, steaming, on the stove downstairs.

Winter's joys are hard fought.

Where summer offers tanned, smiling faces and sun-bleached hair, colder months require us to make do with a rosy touch of color on an icy cheek. Quickly grilled meats are replaced by slowly braised tougher cuts and whole chickens roasting in the oven. Lacking the bright flavors of garden fresh vegetables and fruits, we caramelize root vegetables drawing out their natural sugars.

During these cold months, we layer flavors by sweating aromatics, reducing stocks, and adding bold, complex spices to build richness with winter's simpler ingredients. After hours of cooking, when our efforts finally arrive at a table surrounded by those with whom we shared the day's outdoor adventures, this feels like a victory—even without the crazy dip in an ice-cold stream.

JONATHAN BARDZIK

TIP: Trussing the chicken holds the faster cooking parts of the bird up against the slower cooking body so the whole chicken roasts more evenly.

TIP: When rubbing butter on the chicken, for the first 30 seconds or so it will just slide around before it starts to rub into the skin. Stick with it!

APPLE & GINGER ROAST CHICKEN

Serves 4

Sweet apple and bright ginger add layers of flavor to the crispy skin and juicy meat of this roast chicken. A brandy pan sauce takes it over the top.

For brine:

- 3 tart apples, roughly chopped
- 1 head garlic, peeled
- 6" ginger, peeled and chopped
- 2 cups apple cider
- ½ cup Tamari soy sauce
- 4 cups water
- 1 cup kosher salt
- 1 whole chicken,
      4-4 ½ pounds

For roasting:

- 2" ginger cut in thin rounds
- 1 tart apple, roughly chopped
- 4 sprigs parsley
- 4 cloves peeled garlic
- 4 tbs butter, softened
- 2 tbs olive oil
- 1 ½ pounds Crimini mushrooms, cleaned and quartered
- ¼ cup brandy
- 1 ½ cup chicken stock
- 2 tbs cold butter

Directions:

- For brine, combine apples, garlic, ginger, cider and soy and mix well in blender or food processor. Add to large bowl with water and salt.

- Rinse chicken well and place in brine. If not covered, add additional water. Place in refrigerator for up to 6 hours.

- Remove chicken from brine. Rinse clean, inside and out. Pat dry with paper towels. Stuff cavity with ginger, apple, parsley and garlic.

- Truss chicken. Tie legs together with kitchen twine, closing the cavity. Tuck wings up against the body and secure with twine. Rub with softened butter. Season generously with salt and pepper.

- Preheat oven to 400 degrees, setting rack so the chicken will be about 8" from the heating element.

- Warm oil in a 12" skillet over medium-high heat. Add chicken and brown well on all sides. With chicken breast side down, place skillet in the oven. After 20 minutes, baste chicken and turn breast side up. Add mushrooms and return skillet to oven. Roast 45-60 minutes longer until internal temp of thigh (away from bone) is 165 degrees.

- Remove chicken from oven. Place chicken and mushrooms on a plate, tented with foil, leaving juices in the skillet.

- Skim fat from the pan juices and place the skillet over medium-high heat. Add brandy and reduce, scraping up any brown bits.

- Add stock and reduce by half. Add any accumulated juices from the chicken. Remove skillet from heat and whisk in cold butter. Remove twine, carve and serve with mushrooms and sauce.

THE MAGIC OF THE BRINE

I regularly hear two concerns about brining. First, that it takes too much extra time. Second, that the chicken, or turkey, will be too salty. While, in fairness, brining a chicken does require forethought (several hours ahead of when you plan to put it in the oven), it adds very little work. In this recipe, a food processor does most of the prep and the chicken simply sits around for a few hours.

As for the salt, I don't have a good answer for you. I've read lots of articles and they offer lots of answers from the hypothetical to those measured by a lab. In the end, I haven't found anything definitive, so here's my answer: The meat certainly absorbs some salt, how much is not clear. I do know—from eating lots of brined chickens and turkeys—that they never taste salty. So if your main concern is flavor, brine away, your meat will taste delicious.

WILD RICE CIDER PILAF

Serves 6

Sweet cider and tart cranberries perfectly balance the richness of this native American grain. The rich butter and pecans may tempt you to substitute this pilaf for Thanksgiving's traditional bread stuffing. The answer? Just have both.

Ingredients:

2 cups wild rice
2 cups apple cider
2 sprigs thyme
5 tbs butter
1 onion, diced
1 cup chopped pecans
1 cup dried cranberries
¼ cup chopped parsley

Directions:

- Soak rice in about 6 cups of water for 45–60 minutes. Drain rice and rinse under running water until the water runs clear.

- In a 2 quart saucepan, combine rice with cider, thyme sprigs and a pinch of salt. Cover and bring to a boil. Reduce to low and simmer until liquid is absorbed, 20–30 minutes. Rice should be tender and separate easily with a fork

- Shortly before rice is finished cooking, melt butter in a 10" skillet over medium heat. Add onion and cook until softened, 4–5 minutes.

- Add pecans and cranberries and season lightly with salt and pepper. Cook additional 4 minutes.

- Add parsley and cook 1 minute longer.

- Add cranberry and nut mixture to rice and toss to combine.

- Season to taste with salt and pepper.

TIP: Most wild rice dishes cook for an hour or longer. Soaking significantly cuts down on the cooking time required—a big plus when you're serving this as part of a large holiday meal!

TIP: There are different types of wild rice, some will take longer and be firmer than others. Don't get nervous that you're doing something wrong. Just add more cider or water and keep cooking.

DESPERATION

Certain foods have crossed my plate which raise the question. "Why, in the good Lord's name, did we ever start eating this?" The work involved in harvesting and cooking them is ridiculous and the flavor is just not worth the effort. There are a few exceptions; notably sunchokes, lobster and wild rice.

My discovery that sunchokes can be left unpeeled when roasting, places these nutty, tender roots on the list. Lobster is, well, lobster. Every sweet, firm bite is worth the work of trapping, cooking and removing the meat from the hard shell. It's even worth the smell that stays on your hands for days after.

Wild rice, however, is a tough call. Much of it is still harvested in Minnesota, by canoe, using sticks to knock the rice into the boat. The green grains are then cured and dried before they are ready to cook and eat. Do you just want to beat your head with one of those sticks or is it worth all the hard work?

My answer is a definite "yes." One bite of this dish and I think yours will be, too.

Tip: Pork fat smokes if you look at it the wrong way, never mind when you place it over heat. Fry your bacon over medium-low. And it doesn't hurt to pop open a window or two—just to be safe.

SPINACH & SWEET POTATOES
WITH **BACON VINAIGRETTE**

Serves 8

A hot bacon fat vinaigrette lightly wilts the puckered, dark green leaves of field spinach. Sweet potatoes glazed in tart cider with a bit of spicy cayenne perfectly balance the earthy greens.

Ingredients:

    2 medium sweet potatoes
    1 tbs olive oil
    1 tbs butter
    1 cup apple cider
    White pepper
    Nutmeg
    Cayenne pepper
    3 slices bacon
    1 shallot, minced
    3 tbs jalapeno jelly
    1 tbs grainy mustard
    ⅓ cup cider vinegar
    ½ pound of field spinach

Directions:

- Quarter sweet potatoes lengthwise and cut in thin slices.

- Melt butter together with oil in a 3 quart sauté pan over medium heat. Add potatoes and cook until they begin to brown, about 5 minutes.

- Add cider, cover and cook until sweet potatoes are easily pierced with a fork. Uncover and let any remaining cider reduce to a glaze. Season to taste with salt, white pepper, nutmeg, cayenne and a splash of cider vinegar.

- Meanwhile, cook bacon in a 10" skillet over medium-low heat, browning on both sides. Remove and place on paper towels to drain.

- Add shallot to bacon fat. Increase heat to medium and cook until softened. Add jelly and mustard. When jelly "melts," whisk in cider vinegar.

- Toss spinach and potatoes together. Crumble in bacon. Dress with hot vinaigrette

THE RIGHT SHADE OF GREENS

The first time I cooked dinner for Ray Lavoie was the second time I met him. It may have been the cheap vodka, but something clicked the first time we met, and he invited my husband Jason and me to visit a month later when we traveled to Ohio for Thanksgiving. On the menu that night was spinach salad with a hot bacon fat dressing.

Walking through the grocery store, shopping for ingredients, it occurred to me that I should think carefully about my greens. Baby spinach, I realized, would melt under the hot bacon fat. Beyond their heavier substance, the dark green, earthy, puckered leaves of mature spinach would provide just the right foil for rich, salty bacon fat whisked together with bright, sharp vinegar and sugary melted preserves.

Did I make the right choice? I'd like to think so—and I've certainly been invited back.

TIP: Keep this soup more budget friendly. Use inexpensive Criminis to make up half the volume of wild mushrooms called for in the recipe.

TIP: Criminis, often labeled "baby Bellas" are, in fact, young Portabella mushrooms. Grown five days longer, these brown button mushrooms would turn into the familiar, large, meaty caps.

MUSHROOMY MUSHROOM SOUP

Serves 6–8

Mushroom soup should be bold and earthy, not heavy and bland. Layer upon layer of flavor gives you intense mushroom flavor without cream and flour getting in the way.

Ingredients:

2 tbs olive oil

1 shallot, minced

4 cups chopped wild mushrooms like Crimini, Shitake and Oyster

3–4 sprigs thyme

8–9 cups Rich Mushroom Stock (page 23)

2 tbs butter

2 additional cups thinly sliced wild mushrooms

1 tbs chopped thyme

Freshly grated nutmeg

½ cup Madeira

Sherry vinegar

1 tbs chopped parsley

Directions:

‣ Warm 2 tbs oil in 4 quart saucepan over medium heat.

‣ Add shallot and sauté for 4–5 minutes.

‣ Add 4 cups chopped mushrooms and sauté until lightly brown.

‣ Add thyme sprigs and mushroom stock. Simmer for 20–30 minutes. Strain soup, pressing on solids. Reserve liquid and discard solids.

‣ Melt butter in a sauté pan over medium heat. Add 2 cups sliced mushrooms and sauté until lightly browned and pan is dry. Stir in chopped thyme. Season to taste with salt, pepper and nutmeg. Deglaze pan with Madeira, scraping up any brown bits.

‣ Return mushroom broth to 4 quart saucepan along with sautéed mushrooms. Bring to a simmer and cook for an additional 10 minutes.

‣ Season to taste with vinegar, an additional pat of butter, and salt and pepper. Serve soup garnished with parsley.

IT'S NOT ABOUT THE MONEY

Most mushroom soups offer a few anemic sliced mushrooms suspended in a bland, thin paste of flour and cream. I love mushrooms and wanted a soup that put their rich, earthy taste front and center. The only solution, I discovered, was to use lots of mushrooms.

I began with a rich mushroom stock, enriched with earthy, complex red miso paste. I then simmered that stock with even more mushrooms, before finishing it with freshly sautéed mushrooms, rich and bright with a splash of dry Madeira.

The result? It's not the cheapest soup you will make, but it is loaded with rich mushroom flavor—an elegant first course that is bold enough to make a whole meal accompanied by a salad and a loaf of crusty sourdough with farm-fresh butter.

TIP: Where do you get mushroom stems? When you trim them from Shitakes or button mushrooms, save them in a bag in the freezer. When you have several cups, make a batch of stock. If you don't have enough stems in the freezer, use whole, inexpensive, Crimini mushrooms.

RICH MUSHROOM STOCK

Makes about 2 quarts

Whether braising a pot roast, adding meaty, meat-free richness to vegetarian stews, or making my flavorful Mushroomy Mushroom Soup, this stock adds rich depth and delicious complexity.

Ingredients:

1 tbs olive oil

1 medium onion, chopped

1 large carrot, chopped

1 stalk celery, chopped

2–3 cups chopped mushroom stems

2 tbs red miso paste

½ cup Madeira

4–5 parsley stems

2–3 sprigs thyme

1 bay leaf

1–2 ounces dried Porcini mushrooms

Directions:

- Heat olive oil in a 4 quart saucepan over medium heat. Add onions and sauté for 2–3 minutes.

- Add carrots and celery. Cook for another 5 minutes.

- Add mushroom stems and cook until lightly browned.

- Add miso paste and cook, stirring, for 1 minute.

- Deglaze pan with Madeira, stirring to scrape up brown bits from the bottom of the pan while wine reduces.

- Add parsley stems, thyme springs and bay leaf. Cover with 10 cups water and simmer, partially covered, 30–40 minutes.

- Strain and discard solids. Return stock to simmer.

- Remove from heat and add dried Porcinis. Let sit for 20 minutes.

- Strain through cheese cloth, reserving mushrooms.

TIP: Porcini mushrooms can be a bit dear. Rather than throw them away with the solids, this recipe extracts some flavor, allowing you to save them. If you're making Mushroomy Mushroom Soup or a stew, add the mushrooms to the finished dish.

PUTTING IT TOGETHER: SIMPLE AND HEARTY

On a cold winter night, the darkness oppressive against the windows, snow blowing hard and cold, sometimes you want to skip long, slow roasting or braising and make a simple, hearty meal. Light a candle or sit by the fire and enjoy, safe and warm.

Mushroomy Mushroom Soup
(page 21)
Rosemary Apple Walnut Vinaigrette
(page 47)
A loaf of crusty bread with farm-fresh butter

23

YOU CAN THANK ME LATER

I'll admit it. I'm a stock snob.

I just don't believe that any store-bought stock can measure up to what you make at home. I would rather use a quick homemade vegetable stock than open a can of chicken or beef broth.

Why? It's all about taste. The rich flavor of stock comes from drawing out layers of flavor from fresh ingredients. Commercial stock often skimps on fresh vegetables and meat, making up for them with salt. Even when using low sodium stock, once it's simmered for soup or reduced even further in a sauce, the levels become concentrated again. For the right flavor, I want to control the amount of salt that goes into what I cook.

Fortunately, stock is easy to make. You can have a pot ready by the time you prepare the other ingredients for a Tuesday night dinner. Coarsely chop a carrot, several ribs of celery and an onion. Add a leek if you have one, along with fresh thyme and parsley. Finally, add a few whole peppercorns and a couple of bay leaves, cover the ingredients by two inches with water and simmer for 30–45 minutes. Easy!

But let's say you want chicken stock. No problem! Just add six pounds of the cheapest chicken parts you can find.

If your grocer still cuts up whole chickens into the breasts, wings and thighs they sell, they should have chicken backs and necks left over—and they will sell them to you cheap. Otherwise, just grab whole legs or quarters.

Put the chicken in a pot with your vegetable stock ingredients, bring to a simmer and cook, skimming occasionally, for three hours. Drain the solids, remove the fat and you're done.

This is usually the point when someone says, "Let me tell you about the last time I had three hours to cook something that wasn't ready to eat when I was finished…"

I'm going to make an assumption— about most of you, except my Mom and, well, anyone under 21. Sometime in the next 30 days you're going to wake up on Saturday morning after having had a few too many the night before, and your big plan for the day is to sit on the couch, with a giant cup of coffee, binge watching an entire series on Netflix. And there's just no reason that a big pot of stock can't be quietly simmering away on the stove.

Just think, while curing one hangover, you can make enough stock to freeze and use for several months. Now you can thank me.

VEGETABLE STOCK

Makes about 8 cups

This quick and simple recipe, ready in 30–45 minutes, is my everyday stock. It stores well so keep extra in the freezer for a quick, weeknight soup or flavorful pan sauce.

Ingredients:

1 large carrot (2" diameter and 8" long)
3 ribs celery
1 large onion (about the size of a baseball)
1 leek, white and light green parts only (optional)
1 tsp black peppercorns
2 bay leaves
6–8 parsley stems
4–6 sprigs thyme

Directions:

- Roughly chop the vegetables. This is not the time to practice your fine knife skills. Just cut everything up into big 1–2" chunks.
- Add 10–12 cups water to a 6 quart stock pot. Add all of the ingredients.
- Bring to a simmer over medium–low heat and cook for 45 minutes or so.
- Strain and discard all solids.
- Boil stock and reduce to about 8 cups.

TIP: You can test the level of flavor by putting a little in a small dish and adding a pinch of salt. Taste it. If the flavor is too watery, reduce the stock further.

TIP: Freeze your stock in different sized containers: 6-8 cups will make a pot of soup. A cup will deglaze a skillet and reduce for a delicious pan sauce after sautéing chicken, pork or a steak.

IMPROVISE

Stock is a great way to use vegetable scraps and empty out the fridge, but there are a few guidelines to follow for great flavor. First, if you wouldn't eat it, it doesn't belong in your stock. That emaciated, blackening carrot in the bottom of your vegetable bin is a no-no. This is stock, not compost.

Second, don't add anything too bold or bitter. No peppers and no Brassicas—that includes kale, broccoli, cauliflower and cabbage. To save vegetable trimmings like potato and onion skins or carrot tops, keep a one-gallon bag in the freezer and make a pot of vegetable stock when it's full.

TIP: Letting the chicken cook for 20 minutes before adding the veggies and herbs makes it easier to skim off the foam.

TIP: Buy the cheapest chicken parts you can find. Backs are great. Whole legs and thighs work well, too.

WHITE CHICKEN STOCK

Makes about 8 cups

Chicken stock is easy—and homemade is well worth the effort, mostly dumping a few ingredients into a pot to simmer and skimming it every 30–45 minutes. This keeps in the freezer for months. You'll never use store-bought again!

Ingredients:

6 pounds chicken parts
1 large carrot (2" diameter and 8" long)
3 ribs celery
1 large onion (about the size of a baseball)
1 leek, white parts only (optional)
1 tsp black peppercorns
2 bay leaves
6–8 parsley stems
4–6 sprigs thyme

Directions:

- Cut the chicken into 3 inch pieces. Better yet, have your butcher do it. Place in an 8 quart stock pot and add water to cover the chicken by 2 inches.

- Bring the pot to a simmer over medium heat. Reduce the heat and hold at a slow simmer—just a few bubbles per second.

- Cook the chicken for 15–20 minutes. Skim off the grey/brown foam that gathers on the surface, and discard.

- Meanwhile, roughly chop the vegetables. This is not the time for fine knife skills. Cut everything into 1–2" chunks.

- Add the rest of the ingredients to the stock pot and continue to simmer for three hours. Don't let your stock come above a simmer. Boiling stock will emulsify the fat and make it cloudy. But if it does, don't worry. It will still taste delicious!

- At the end of three hours, remove and discard the solids. Then strain your stock through a fine mesh sieve.

- Remove the fat from the stock by cooling it to room temperature and refrigerating it overnight. The fat will congeal on the surface and is easily removed. If you need the stock right away, let it rest for 15–20 minutes. The fat will float to the surface of the stock and you can remove it with a spoon.

- If the stock is too thin or bland, reduce it down to 8 cups over a gentle boil.

WHAT'S SO WHITE ABOUT THIS STOCK?

What makes white stock white? White stock begins with raw meat and vegetables added directly to the stock pot. The other kind of stock, brown, uses meat and veggies that have been roasted, or browned, first.

What's the difference? Think about steaming or roasting asparagus. The steamed asparagus is tender and mild in flavor. The roasted asparagus brings out richness and natural sugars. Brown stocks, just like the asparagus, have fuller, bolder flavor.

If you are making soup or sauces with delicate vegetables and meat, use white stock. For rich hearty soups, like a winter chicken, or saucing a roast, choose brown stock for richer flavor.

TIP: Unlike flavorful chicken bones, you need the extra meat to
make beef stock bold and flavorful. It's not cheap, but good
homemade beef stock is delicious!

BEEF STOCK

Makes about 8 cups

Sure, it is expensive and time consuming, but just I haven't found a flavorful beef stock on the grocery shelf that isn't mostly salt. Homemade will blow your mind and is worth making just to fill your home with the aroma of roasting meat.

Ingredients:

8 pounds beef meat and bones, I usually use 4 pounds
      bone-in short ribs and 4 pounds oxtail

1 large carrot (2" diameter and 8" long)

3 ribs celery

1 large onion (about the size of a baseball)

1 leek, white parts only (optional)

3 tbs tomato paste

1 cup dry red wine

1 tsp black peppercorns

2 bay leaves

6–8 parsley stems

1–6 sprigs thyme

Directions:

- Place the beef in a single layer in a roasting pan that can be used later on the stovetop. Roast about 50 minutes at 400 degrees until browned, turning once. If needed, use two pans or cook in two batches. Place roasted bones in an 8 quart stock pot.

- Roughly chop the vegetables into 1-2" chunks. Place in roasting pan and cook for 45 minutes. Toss with tomato paste and return to oven for 15 minutes longer. Add roasted vegetables to pot with beef.

- Place roasting pan on stove over medium-high heat. Add wine, if it doesn't cover the bottom of the pan, add a cup or two of water. Reduce liquid by half, scraping up brown bits from the bottom of the pan. Add to stock pot with beef and vegetables along with spices and herbs. Cover ingredients by two inches with water.

- Bring the pot to a simmer over medium heat. Reduce heat to hold at a slow simmer—just a few bubbles per second. Every 30 minutes, skim any foam from the surface. At the end of eight hours, remove and discard solids. Strain stock through a fine mesh sieve.

- Remove fat from stock by cooling to room temperature and refrigerating overnight. The fat will congeal on the surface and is easily removed. If you need the stock right away, let it rest for 15-20 minutes and remove fat with a spoon. If the stock is too thin or bland, reduce down to 8 cups at a gentle boil.

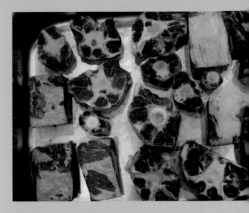

CRUEL AND UNUSUAL

Making beef stock means filling your home for 8–10 hours with the rich smell of roasting beef—and at the end there is nothing ready to eat. My husband Jason calls this cruel and unusual torture. So we've come to an agreement. Every time I make beef stock, I've got to cook some beef, anything from a quick skirt steak to slow braised short ribs.

If you're tempted to use the left over beef from the stock, learn from the error of my ways. I'll admit, it seems like a lot of beef and looks like it should be okay to eat, but by the time your stock is finished there is no flavor left. I made the mistake—just once—of cooking it up with lots of onion, garlic, freshly toasted ground cumin and chile powder. The results? Gross. It was like fajita seasoned, meat-textured cardboard. Just. Don't. Trust me.

TIP: White pepper has a lighter, more floral flavor than black peppercorns, making it a perfect pairing with the light, starchy flavor of celery root. Just like black, white pepper is best freshly cracked.

CELERY ROOT SOUP WITH BACON & APPLE

Serves 6–8

Creamy and rich, with a bright hint of celery and almost no cream.
The garnishes take this soup from good to spectacular.

Ingredients:

2 strips thick cut bacon, diced

4 shallots, minced

1 large celery root, diced

1 clove garlic, minced

8 cups vegetable stock, divided (page 27)

2 tbs cream

2 tbs butter

Sherry vinegar

White pepper

Pinch nutmeg

1 tart apple cut in thin matchsticks

1 rib celery, thinly sliced

Celery leaves, chopped

Directions:

‣ Place bacon in a 4 quart stock pot over medium-low heat. Cook until bacon is brown and fat is rendered. Remove bacon with slotted spoon and place on paper towel to drain.

‣ Add shallots to pan with bacon fat and sauté over medium heat until soft. Add celery root and cook additional 3–5 minutes. Add garlic and cook 1 minute until fragrant.

‣ Add 2 cups stock and stew, partially covered, for 5–7 minutes.

‣ Add remaining stock and simmer 10–15 minutes longer until celery root is soft.

‣ Process soup with an immersion blender or food processor until smooth.

‣ Return soup to pot and warm to a simmer over medium heat.

‣ Remove the soup from heat and stir in the cream and butter. Season to taste with salt, white pepper, nutmeg and vinegar.

‣ Serve garnished with apple matchsticks, celery, celery leaves and crumbled bacon.

THE WORLD'S UGLIEST VEGETABLE

Celery root may be the world's ugliest vegetable, all rough and grey, one end a messy tangle of roots and dirt. The root end is the bottom, while from the knob on top grows a bitter relative of the familiar celery you fill with cream cheese for snacking.

To prepare it for cooking, take a thick slice off the root end. This is painful for thrifty New Englanders who hope against hope that they can clean around the nubby roots with a peeler or pairing knife. These are the same people who take the hard brown dots off a thinly peeled pineapple using a grapefruit spoon. They are either deeply committed or have a lot of free time. (I love you Mom!)

Once you cut off the root end, peel the brown-grey skin revealing the white, starchy interior. Celery root is great roasted, or boiled and mashed with potatoes. The outer ugly duckling truly reveals a beautiful, and delicious, swan inside.

TIP: Masa harina has a unique flavor distinct from corn meal.
   If you can't find it in your grocery store or Spanish market,
   make 1/4 cup of crumbs by pulsing a corn tortilla or two
   in the food processor.

VEGETARIAN TORTILLA SOUP

Serves 8

Bright, rich and complex. The blend of dried chiles delivers an earthy, hot and sweet foundation for tomatoes and fresh herbs. This stick-to-your-ribs, meat-free goodness will warm you through on the coldest, raw winter day.

Ingredients:

1 Ancho chile
2 Guajillo chiles
2 Arbol chiles
2 cloves garlic, chopped
1 onion, diced
1 can San Marzano tomatoes (about 28 ounces)
1 tbs cumin seed, toasted
1 bunch cilantro
2 tbs epazote
4 tbs olive oil, divided
8–10 cups vegetable stock (page 27)
1 tbs masa harina
1 corn tortilla, cut in thin strips
1 tsp chili powder
1 cup queso fresco or mild feta cheese
Sherry vinegar
1 avocado, sliced thinly
1 lime, cut in wedges

Directions:

- Toast chiles in a dry pan over medium heat for 3 minutes per side. Place in a pot of boiling water and cook for 10 minutes.

- Remove chiles, cool and seed. Place in food processor with garlic, onion, tomatoes, toasted cumin seed, 3–4 sprigs cilantro and epazote. Purée until smooth.

- Warm 2 tbs olive oil in a 4 quart soup pot over medium heat. Add purée and simmer for 7–10 minutes until thickened.

- Add stock and masa to purée and cook for 15 minutes, stirring frequently.

- Meanwhile, toss tortilla strips in remaining 2 tbs olive oil and chili powder. Toast in a 400 degree oven.

- Add cheese to soup and warm for 5 minutes. Season to taste with salt, pepper and vinegar. Serve topped with tortilla strips, avocado, lime wedges and chopped cilantro.

PURSUING PEPPERS

More and more ingredients common in Central and South American cooking are available in grocery stores, often in the international aisle. The three dried chiles in this soup are: Ancho, which gives mild heat and sweetness; wrinkled, dark Guajillo, with an almost raisin-y flavor; and little red Arboles, for a pleasant kick. If you can't find the less-common Arboles, season to taste with a pinch of cayenne.

Epazote, also called Mexican oregano, has a distinct earthy flavor that is irreplaceable. However, if you can't find it, go ahead and use dried oregano or summer savory. You'll still have a great pot of soup!

PORTUGUESE KALE & SAUSAGE SOUP

Serves 6

So simple, so delicious! Rich potatoes, spicy sausage and hearty kale. The first time I made this soup, my husband Jason and I shoved down our bowlfuls as fast as we could to go back for seconds.

Ingredients:

2 tbs olive oil
2 Spanish chorizo, Portuguese linguiça, or
    Polish kielbasa sausages, diced small
1 medium onion, diced
2 cloves garlic, minced
4 medium starchy potatoes, like Russet or Eva, thinly sliced
6 cups chicken or vegetable stock, divided (pages 29 and 27)
2 bay leaves
4 sprigs thyme
1 pound Lacinato kale, ribs removed
2 tbs butter
Sherry vinegar

Directions:

- In a 4 quart saucepan over medium heat, sauté diced sausage in olive oil until lightly browned. Remove sausage with slotted spoon, leaving fat in the pan.
- Add onions to pan and cook until softened. Add garlic, potatoes and 1 cup of stock. Decrease heat to medium-low and stew for 10 minutes.
- Add remaining stock, bay leaves and thyme sprigs. Simmer until potatoes can be easily mashed.
- Roughly mash the potatoes in the soup. Add sausage and simmer for 5 minutes.
- Meanwhile, stack your kale leaves in bunches of 5–6, roll them tightly, like a cigar, and slice across to cut them in thin ribbons.
- Add kale to soup and simmer 5 minutes longer.
- Season to taste with butter, vinegar, salt and pepper.

TIP: Good greens are all about texture. Cutting your kale into thin ribbons—a chiffonade—makes the mouthfeel more delicate and less like you're chewing on coarse clippings from the front lawn.

A PINCH OF SALT

Four years ago, my boss at the time, Bob, walked into my office. "My wife Susie and I have a CSA—a farm share," Bob said. "Its fall and we're getting lots of greens. I hate them, but my doctor says they are good for me, so I'm dutifully eating them." That's Bob.

"Bob," I asked, "How are you cooking your greens?" He described soups, salads and sautés that all sounded delicious. "And how are you seasoning them, Bob?" I asked. He mentioned fresh herbs and bright spices. Perplexed, I finally said, "How about salt?"

Bob recoiled, "Oh no! Salt is bad for you. We don't use salt."

"Bob," I replied, "savory dishes will never taste good without a little salt."

The unhealthy amounts of salt in our diet come from packaged, processed and prepared foods, not farm and garden-fresh ingredients. In fact, home cooked food will taste inedibley over-salted before you make it unhealthy.

So put down the fast-food burger, leave the chips of the shelf and add a pinch of salt to your kale. It's healthy. And, more importantly, delicious.

Tip: Red miso is a bolder flavored paste than the traditional white and yellow. The red color comes from a higher ratio of soybeans to grains and longer fermentation. It is bold, funky and delicious, and adds that "je ne sais quoi" complexity that is often missing from meatless soups.

CAULIFLOWER KALE TOMATO SOUP

Serves 8–10

This bold complex vegetable soup builds layer upon layer of flavor—earthy, caramelized mushrooms, sweet, rich tomato paste, smoky paprika and salty miso. You'll never miss the meat!

Ingredients:

  2 tbs olive oil
  2 Portabella mushrooms, diced
  2 cups sliced Crimini mushrooms
  1 large onion, diced
  3 cloves garlic, minced
  2 tbs tomato paste
  1 tbs red miso paste
  2 tbs sweet paprika
  1 cup dry white wine
  2 bay leaves
  2 sprigs thyme
  8 cups vegetable stock (page 27)
  1 medium head cauliflower, cut in florets
  3 beefsteak tomatoes, cut in 2" dice
  10 cups Portuguese kale, chopped
  2 tbs butter
  Red wine vinegar

Directions:

- Heat oil in an 8 quart soup pot over medium-high heat. Add mushrooms and cook 5–7 minutes until beginning to brown. Add onions and cook until softened. Add garlic and cook 1 minute until fragrant.

- Add tomato paste, red miso paste and paprika. Cook 1 minute until fragrant. Add wine and deglaze pan, scraping up any brown bits.

- Add bay leaves, thyme sprigs and vegetable stock. Simmer 10 minutes, allowing flavors to develop.

- Add cauliflower, kale and tomatoes. Cook until cauliflower is just tender.

- Season soup to taste with a pat of butter, a splash of vinegar, salt and pepper.

A CHRISTMAS MIRACLE

My sister Katie has two beautiful, amazing, young children (who take after their uncle). They are at an age that makes precise scheduling a challenge. This year, knowing that Katie would be driving up to our family's home on Christmas day, my Dad suggested we postpone our multi-course dinner to the day after and instead keep a couple of pots of soup simmering on the stove that we could tuck into at any time.

His idea was inspired and made for a wonderfully relaxed Christmas day. It also delivered a Christmas miracle. My niece and nephew pushed aside their organic, free-range, antibiotic-free, cruelty-free, multi-lingual, Ivy League-educated chicken nuggets in favor of a simple bowl filled with whole ingredients and fresh vegetables. It was truly the best Christmas gift ever.

OPENIN' A CAN OF SOMETHING

There's a tradition in my friend Ellen's family. Each year, on your birthday, you get to choose what is served for dinner. Every March, Ellen chooses spaghetti.

It may seem like a simple choice, but Ellen grew up on a farm and everything her family ate was raised or grown there, from chickens and eggs to fresh veggies. By March, the winter's canned goods began to run low and there were never more than three jars of the previous summer's tomatoes remaining in the pantry. Ellen knew that if she asked for spaghetti, her mother would take one of those precious jars down off the shelf to make a pot of sauce.

Lacking the home-preserved perfection of Ellen's mother's tomatoes, I turn to another source. First, I should warn you, if you picked up this book expecting to find a purist, a strict evangelist for farm and garden-fresh food without exception, you're about to be disappointed.

While they are few and carefully chosen, I do keep canned goods on hand. Coconut milk and curry paste offer a quick and delicious way to avoid expensive takeout, while artichokes and olives dress up a late-night pot of pasta. However, the most prized canned ingredient in my winter pantry is San Marzano tomatoes.

San Marzanos are the Champagne of canned tomatoes. To receive their official status, displayed proudly on the can by the letters "D.O.P.", this specific breed of thin-skinned, Italian heirloom, plum tomatoes must be grown in the Sarno valley near Naples.

Why does that make them so special? Some swear by the climate and others the water, but everyone seems to agree that the minerals found in the ash-rich soil near Mount Vesuvius, where they grow, make San Marzanos the most delicious tomatoes in the world.

So, this next March, if Ellen can't make it home, I just may drop by with a can of San Marzanos and make a big bowl of spaghetti for her birthday. I'll bring a few bottles of Champagne, too.

ANDOUILLE SWORDFISH STEW

Serves 6

Bright with tomatoes, hearty from meaty swordfish, with just the right touch of heat from spicy Andouille sausage, this lighter alternative to beef stew sacrifices none of the satisfaction.

Ingredients:

4 tbs olive oil, divided

1 andouille sausage, quartered and cut in ½" slices

2 medium onions, halved and thinly sliced

3 cloves garlic, minced

4 cups fingerling potatoes, cut in 1" pieces

1 ½ cups dry white wine

1 14 ounce can San Marzano or other plum tomatoes

3 bay leaves

1 tbs dried oregano

1 ½ pounds swordfish steak, 1" thick, skinned and cut in 1" cubes

2 tbs chopped rosemary, divided

Directions:

‣ Warm 2 tbs olive oil in a heavy bottomed soup pot over medium heat. Add sausage and cook until browned. Remove with slotted spoon.

‣ Add onions and cook until softened and beginning to brown. Add garlic and cook 1 minute longer.

‣ Add potatoes and cook for five minutes.

‣ Add wine, partially cover, and stew until liquid is reduced by half.

‣ Add tomatoes, bay leaves, oregano and cooked sausage. Cover and cook until potatoes are easily split with a knife, about 10–20 minutes.

‣ Add swordfish and stir in 1 tbs rosemary. Cover and cook 10–12 minutes until fish is cooked through.

‣ Stir in remaining 2 tbs olive oil and 1 tbs rosemary, and season to taste with salt and pepper.

TIP: Adding some of the rosemary earlier in the cooking gives mellow depth to the dish while sprinkling in a bit more at the end lends a bright, piney punch.

PUTTING IT TOGETHER: APRÈS

Whether your afternoon was spent skiing, snowshoeing or shoveling, there is a particular joy in coming indoors, rosy-cheeked, from a day spent outside with bright, cold sun reflecting off new snow. It's time to enjoy dinner at a table surrounded by family and good friends, in a home warmed by a crackling fire and bright laughter. Keep it simple with a selection of soups and a hearty salad.

Andouille Swordfish Stew
Cauliflower Kale Tomato Soup (page 39)
Vegetarian Tortilla Soup (page 35)
Spinach and Sweet Potatoes with Bacon Vinaigrette (page 19)
Warm a crusty loaf of bread in the oven and serve it with lots of farm-fresh butter

TIP: Capers are the flower buds of the caper berry plant, Capparis spinosa. The larger ones have better flavor, but the smaller, non-pareil ones are firmer. They can be packed in salt or brined in salt water. Connoisseurs will argue for salt-packed, but rinsing them takes a little more work. Bottom line—there is a difference, but they are all delicious!

MUSHROOM TAPENADE

Makes 1–1½ cups

Cheaper and less briny than olive tapenade, this crowd-pleaser is earthy, comforting and versatile. Serve it with toasted slices of baguette or as a sauce over baked white fish or sautéed pork chops.

Ingredients:

    4 tbs butter, divided
    2 large shallots, minced (about ½ cup)
    1 clove garlic, minced
    1 tsp anchovy paste
    4 cups chopped wild mushrooms, like Crimini, Shitake,
        Oyster or Chanterelle
    2 tbs olive oil—the good stuff!
    2 tbs capers, rinsed and minced
    1 tbs chopped oregano
    1 tbs chopped parsley
    Fresh squeezed lemon juice

Directions:

- Melt 2 tbs butter in a large sauté pan over medium-low heat. Add shallot and cook until softened, about 5 minutes.

- Add garlic and anchovy paste. Cook until fragrant, about 1 minute.

- Increase heat to medium and add remaining 2 tbs butter. When butter is melted, add mushrooms and cook until softened and golden, about 8–10 minutes.

- Add capers, oregano and parsley. Stir through and cook until fragrant, about 1 minute.

- Season to taste with salt, pepper and a squeeze of lemon juice.

TIP: When sautéing mushrooms, make sure your pan is hot and don't crowd them. Heat the pan for 2–3 minutes over medium-high and cook the mushrooms in multiple batches, if needed. Otherwise, you'll end up with a panful of watery, braised mushrooms.

EWWWWWW!

You're freaked about the anchovy paste, aren't you? Your nose is wrinkled in disgust at the thought of it—fishy, salty and grey, oozing like toothpaste from a tube. Anchovy paste adds necessary and magical layers of flavor in a dish that might otherwise be one-dimensional. You won't taste it, I promise. It's one of those perfect stealth ingredients, delivering lots of flavor without getting caught. So go ahead, squeeze a bit in, and don't tell your kids or your picky eater of a boyfriend. They'll never know.

*Yes, you've read this before. I used it in my first book. But it's the perfect description of anchovy paste. So I used it again.

ROSEMARY APPLE WALNUT VINAIGRETTE

Makes 1 cup of dressing

Sharp, cider vinegar, piney rosemary and rich, toasted walnut oil combine to create what may be the best dressing ever for winter greens, fresh from the cold frame. Serve it over bright, peppery arugula or pleasantly bitter mesclun.

Ingredients:

1 clove garlic, minced
⅓ cup cider vinegar
1 tbs honey
1 tsp grainy mustard
1 tsp minced rosemary
⅓ cup olive oil—the good stuff!
⅓ cup toasted walnut oil

Directions:

- Sprinkle minced garlic with coarse salt and mash into paste on your cutting board using the flat edge of your knife. Place in a medium bowl.
- Add vinegar, honey, mustard and rosemary to bowl with garlic. Season with fresh cracked pepper and let sit for 5–10 minutes for flavors to develop.
- While whisking, drizzle oil into vinegar mixture to form a thick, creamy emulsion.
- Season to taste with additional salt, pepper and vinegar.

TIP: Start chopping rosemary slowly—or the rounded needles will jump right off the cutting board!

A GIFT OF MYRRH

Carefully guard your love for food and cooking. Once revealed to family and friends, food gifts begin to appear from frustrated holiday shoppers. At some point this means bottles of flavored oils and vinegars that you have no idea what to do with or seem too special to use.

This gave rise to a lovely tradition. Every year I would graciously receive a bottle each of oil and vinegar with effusive thanks (my mother raised me right). One year later the giver would present another set. I would remove the previous year's gift from my cabinet and replace old with new.

Then I began developing recipes for a local oil and vinegar store and learned that these specialty products are really easy to use. Just taste them and think: What dish would benefit from the herbal flavor of this basil-infused oil? Is your vinegar sweet? Dress baby spinach. Sharp and bold? Brighten beef stew or tomato sauce with a splash.

They may be too special to use, but they are far too delicious to waste.

TIP: The bone in your pork shoulder roast will add lots of extra
flavor during those long hours in the oven. However, if you
can't find one with a bone, you'll still have a delicious dinner!

CIDER-BRAISED PORK SHOULDER WITH CARAMELIZED ONIONS

Serves 6–8

Layer upon layer of sweet mild flavors make this roast delicious and complex. Be ready to fight over the sauce!

Ingredients:

    3–4 pound bone-in pork shoulder roast
    3 cloves garlic, thinly sliced
    ½ tsp ground cardamom
    2 tbs olive oil
    2 large onions, halved and thinly sliced
    2 tbs brown sugar
    3–4 cups apple cider
    ¼ cup Tamari soy sauce
    ¼ cup cider vinegar
    1 tbs butter
    ¼ cup chopped parsley

Directions:

- Cut thin slits all over pork and insert garlic slices. Season pork with salt, pepper and cardamom and rub into surface of meat.

- Heat olive oil in a Dutch oven over medium-high heat. Add roast and sear on all sides, about 3 minutes per side. Remove from pot and set aside.

- Add onions to hot Dutch oven and sprinkle with salt. After 10 minutes, reduce heat to medium and cook an additional 10 minutes until onions are deeply browned. Sprinkle with sugar.

- Add cider, soy sauce and vinegar to pot and stir to blend. Add pork, fat side up. Liquid should come just over half way up the side of the pork. Add more cider if needed.

- Bring liquid to a boil then transfer pork to a 250 degree oven. Cook for 4–6 hours until center registers 140 degrees. Remove pork from pot and let sit on a platter, loosely tented with foil.

- Skim fat from the sauce, using a fat separator if desired. Reduce by two-thirds.

- Whisk in butter and serve over sliced pork. Sprinkle with parsley.

PUTTING IT TOGETHER: MID-WINTER WARM SNAP

You know that one week in January that offers the false hope of spring? For a few balmy days you unzip your jacket and even go jogging in shorts. While the cold will return, it's the perfect time for a lighter-tasting winter meal, enjoyed with lungs full of fresh air and scarf-wrapped snowmen out in the yard.

Cider-braised Pork Shoulder with Caramelized Onions

Wild Rice Cider Pilaf (page 17)

Bleu Mashed Rutabaga & Potato (page 71)

I ♥ JASON

I kept Julia Child next to my bed for an entire year. Her cookbook, I mean, not her. That would be weird. I read a few pages of *Mastering the Art of French Cooking* each morning and another recipe or two every night.

I woke up on Valentine's Day that year and decided it was time I learned how to make a soufflé. Turning to the chapter on entrées and luncheon dishes, I read the recipe out loud to my husband Jason. In it, Julia mentions the copper bowls French chefs favor for whisking egg whites. Using them, she claims, creates a third more volume than egg whites whisked in conventional bowls with cream of tartar.

While Jason jumped in the shower, I headed downstairs to the kitchen. Passing through the living room I saw the pound of Belgian chocolates I'd bought for him sitting next to a large vase filled with an arm-load of flowers I had carried home and hand-arranged.

Now, Jason and I have no *quid pro quo* about gifts. There's no expectation that each person's pile of gifts will reach the same height or cost the same amount of money. If we see something we think will make the other happy, we just buy it. However, as he had not bought me anything yet, Jason was making out pretty well this particular Valentine's Day.

Thirty minutes later, thanks to Julia's brilliantly simple and clear recipe, my soufflé was already rising in the oven when Jason walked in looking a bit sheepish. He handed me a folded sheet of paper from our computer printer. I opened it to find a picture of the copper beating bowl he had just ordered for me, and fell in love all over again.

My husband is even smarter than he appears. Not only did he come up with the perfect Valentine's save, but when the copper bowl arrived two weeks later, he got another soufflé out of the deal.

And, yes, it was a third higher.

TIP: There are three components to a soufflé—the Béchamel sauce and egg yolks, the stiff egg whites, and your flavoring. Add a cup of whatever you want—corn and cheddar, smoked salmon and gruyere, or pulled pork and kale. Have fun and experiment. You'll never go wrong.

MANCHEGO SERRANO SOUFFLÉ

Serves 4-6

This is the first soufflé I ever made. Dozens later, it has never failed me. The ingredients are nothing more than pantry staples, making this an easy go-to for entertaining or a quick weeknight supper, served with greens dressed in a hand-whisked vinaigrette.

Ingredients:

3 tbs unsalted butter, plus additional to butter soufflé dish

3 tbs finely grated Parmesan cheese

3 tbs all-purpose flour, unbleached

1 cup whole milk

White pepper

Cayenne pepper

Nutmeg

4 large egg yolks

5 large egg whites

½ cup grated Manchego cheese

½ cup diced jamón Serrano (Serrano ham)

Directions:

- Heat oven to 400 degrees. Adjust the rack so the top of the soufflé dish will be about 8" from the heating element. Butter the inside of a 2 quart soufflé dish. Add grated Parmesan and turn dish to coat, reserving extra cheese.

- Béchamel sauce: Melt butter in a small saucepan over medium-low heat. Add flour and stir for 2-3 minutes, being careful not to brown.

- Remove from heat and add milk all at once, whisking vigorously to avoid lumps.

- Return the sauce to medium-low heat and cook for 3-5 minutes until very thick. Season to taste with salt, white pepper and a pinch each of cayenne and nutmeg. Stir the egg yolks into the sauce one at a time.

- Whisk the egg whites to stiff peaks in a freshly cleaned bowl.

- In a large bowl, combine the Béchamel sauce with the cheese and jamón. Stir in ¼ of the stiff egg whites.

- Gently fold in the remaining ¾ of the egg whites until only a few streaks remain. Transfer to the prepared soufflé dish, smooth out the top with a spatula and sprinkle with remaining Parmesan.

- Place in the oven, reduce heat to 375 degrees, and bake for 25 minutes. The soufflé is done when top is golden brown and moves slightly in the middle. I prefer mine still wet in the center.

HOW A SOUFFLÉ RISES

When you whisk your egg whites to stiff peaks, you are suspending air between the strong protein strands. Once in the oven, that air expands before the egg cooks and sets, giving the soufflé its distinctive rise.

The reason we fold the egg whites gently into the batter is to keep as much of that air as possible suspended in the egg white, giving us a fluffier, taller rise and creating a delicate, light dish. Stirring in ¼ of the egg whites before folding in the rest lightens the batter to retain even more air. Don't open the door for the first 20 minutes it's in the oven. But don't worry about tiptoeing around the kitchen. I've never had a soufflé fall in the oven.

However, be prepared because the soufflé will fall in just a minute or two once it comes out. Warn your guests ahead of time so they are seated at the table and can witness your creation in all it's glory!

NEARLY SICILIAN FENNEL ORANGE SALAD

Serves 4

This is my take on a Sicilian classic. Light, fresh fennel and sweet, winter oranges get an earthy, salty bite from Kalamata olives and a bright red wine vinaigrette. You'll almost believe it's spring.

For dressing:

- 1 small shallot, minced
- ½ tsp dried oregano
- ¼ tsp orange zest
- ¼ cup red wine vinegar
- ½ cup olive oil—the good stuff!

For salad:

- 1 medium bulb fennel
- 2 oranges
- 1 shallot, thinly sliced in rounds
- ¼ cup Kalamata olives, quartered

Directions:

- Remove fronds from fennel bulb and reserve. Cut fennel bulb in quarters, remove the core and thinly slice.

- Remove the top and bottom from the orange, exposing the flesh. Slice down the sides, removing all of the rind and the white pith underneath. Over a bowl, carefully slice between the membranes, releasing the fruit. These pieces of orange are called supremes.

- Begin dressing: Whisk together minced shallot, oregano, orange zest, vinegar and a pinch of salt and pepper. Stir in any juice from the bowl of orange supremes. Set aside.

- Combine fennel, oranges, sliced shallot and olives in large bowl with 2 tbs of chopped fennel fronds.

- Finish dressing: While whisking, drizzle oil into vinegar mixture. This will form a creamy emulsion.

- Taste the dressing with a piece of fennel. Season dressing to taste with additional salt, pepper and vinegar.

- Toss salad in ¼ cup of dressing. Add additional dressing to taste.

IF YOU HATE BLACK LICORICE

If you hate black jelly beans, you may be disconcerted to discover that fennel has a light, licoricey taste. However, before you dismiss it, remember that basil—which you likely love—also has a light, licoricey backnote to it. So, rather than say, "I hate licorice, I should probably never try fennel," think, "I love basil, fennel may taste really good."

Then try tarragon and chervil. Just ask my husband Jason. He loves fennel but each Easter can be found picking the black jelly beans, one by one, from his basket.

TIP: Cutting oranges into supremes can be a lot of work, especially if they are soft. You can also slice your oranges into rounds, across the center, making them look like wagon wheels.

Tip: Scraping the pan as the wine bubbles away will not only
return all that crusty, brown goodness to the sauce, but clean
your pan at the same time.

HERB-CRUSTED PORK CHOPS WITH **PARSNIPS**

Serves 4

Simple, quick and easy, this one-dish dinner shows off winter's hearty root vegetables and rich mushrooms at their best with fresh herbs from the windowsill.

Ingredients:

- 3 tbs olive oil
- 2 large parsnips, cut in ¼" dice
- ¼ pound pancetta, diced
- 4 bone-in pork chops
- 2 tbs chopped rosemary
- 2 tbs chopped thyme
- ¼ cup chopped parsley
- 2 cups roughly chopped Maitake or halved Crimini mushrooms
- 1 shallot, minced
- ¼ cup dry white wine

Directions:

- Heat oven to 375 degrees.
- In a baking dish, toss parsnips with 1 tbs olive oil, salt and pepper. Spread in a single layer and roast until tender, about 45 minutes.
- Pat pork chops dry and rub both sides with oil. Season with salt and pepper.
- Toss together fresh herbs. Press 1 tbs of herb mixture onto each side of each pork chop.
- Sauté pancetta in a 12" oven-safe pan over medium heat, about 5–7 minutes. Remove pancetta with a slotted spoon and drain on paper towels.
- Return pan to medium-high heat. Add pork chops and brown on both sides, about 5 minutes per side.
- Add mushrooms to pan and place in oven. Cook to 140 degrees, about 15 minutes. Remove to plate and tent with foil.
- Drain all but 1 tbs fat from pan and return to medium heat. Add shallot and cook until softened. Deglaze pan with wine, scraping up brown bits while wine reduces by half.
- Toss pancetta and roast parsnips in the pan with wine. Serve with pork and mushrooms.

WHAT WINE DO YOU COOK WITH?

I am often asked what white wine to cook with. Once upon a time Jason, my husband, and I received the advice that we should use leftover wine. We turned to each other, perplexed, asking, what is "leftover" wine? I'm pretty sure we've never opened a bottle we haven't finished that night.

Next, someone suggested, "Keep something dry in the pantry just for cooking, like a good Sauvignon Blanc." The problem is—and I know you've been there—it's the end of the night, you've drunk every last drop of wine in the house, and you need just one more glass. Suddenly that bottle of cooking wine is gone.

So, the one bottle we've found we can reliably keep around is dry Vermouth. After all, waving the bottle over a martini glass for a dry cocktail doesn't use very much. So that is what we cook with.

TIP: To get a good sear on your pot roast, your pan will have
to be nice and hot. Let it warm up until the bacon fat
sends up the first wisp of smoke.

MUSHROOM & TURNIP POT ROAST

Serves 6–8

Slow cooked turnips taste like potatoes with a wonderful little extra kick, while mushrooms and homemade stock give this cheap, tender cut of meat, rich, deep flavor.

Ingredients:

    3 strips bacon
    3 pound pot roast
    1 cup diced Crimini mushrooms
    1 onion, diced
    1 carrot, diced
    2 ribs celery, diced
    ½ cup dry red wine
    3 cups beef or mushroom stock (pages 31 and 23)
    2 bay leaves
    2 sprigs thyme
    2 tbs chopped rosemary
    2 cups sliced Crimini mushrooms
    2 turnips, cut in 2" chunks

Directions:

- Fry bacon in a Dutch oven over medium heat. Remove bacon with a slotted spoon, leaving fat in pot.

- Season roast with salt and pepper. Increase heat to medium-high and sear roast on all sides. Remove and reserve on plate.

- If pan is dry, add 2 tbs olive oil. Add diced mushrooms and cook until brown on edges. Add onions and cook 5 minutes until translucent. Add carrots and celery and cook 5 minutes longer.

- Add red wine and deglaze pot, scraping up any brown bits. Return beef and bacon to pot with stock, bay leaves, thyme sprigs and rosemary. Bring to a boil, cover and simmer until fork tender, about 3 hours.

- Add sliced mushrooms and turnips to pot. Cover and cook 50–60 minutes longer until turnips are tender.

- Remove beef and vegetables from pot. Reduce broth by half and serve over beef.

CROCKPOT COOKING

Crockpots are a wonderful way to braise or slowly simmer food without hogging the oven or while you are out of the house. To use them, however, you've got to start on the stove.

Searing, deglazing and reducing are critical steps in building a foundation of flavor for soups, stews and braises. These require a heavy bottomed pot and the heat of your stovetop. Once you've seared the meat, cooked down your onions a bit, then added liquid and scraped up all the beautiful brown bits on the bottom of the pot you can transfer the whole operation over to a crockpot for the next 6-8 hours to finish cooking.

To use a crockpot with any of the recipes in this book, look for the point where it says "cook for the next several hours…" That's where you transfer your ingredients from the stovetop.

QUICK SAUTÉED KALE WITH CRANBERRIES

Serves 6

I usually like my veggies lightly cooked and still fresh-tasting, but getting kale tender without slow cooking proved a challenge. Here's the solution, ready—including chopping—in under 15 minutes.

Ingredients:

2 tbs olive oil
1 shallot, minced
1 pound kale, de-ribbed and cut into thin ribbons
2 tsp sugar
2 tbs balsamic vinegar
½ cup dried cranberries

Directions:

- Heat oil in a 12" skillet over medium heat. Add shallot and sauté until softened 2–3 minutes.

- Turn heat to medium-high and add ¼ of the kale. Sprinkle with a pinch of sugar and a pinch of salt. When the kale just begins to wilt, about 30 seconds, add another ¼. Repeat with the remaining kale.

- After adding the last ¼ of the kale, toss with vinegar and cook 1 minute longer, allowing vinegar to reduce.

- Serve tossed with dried cranberries.

TIP: To de-rib the kale, fold the leaves in half along the rib, and tear it free. To thinly slice the greens, stack several and roll them the long way, like a cigar, then slice thinly across the roll.

TIP: Kale can taste too bitter and grassy for some palates. The dried fruit and pinches of sugar combat the bitter flavors while the vinegar brightens the grassy notes.

PUTTING IT TOGETHER: A WEEKEND AT THE CABIN

You wake up early, sun streaming in the window, brisk breezes blowing outside. Today's plan is to enjoy a lazy breakfast over slowly sipped cups of coffee and much conversation. An afternoon spent snowshoeing and cross-country skiing will build an appetite for tender, falling apart meat that has spent hours slow-cooking in the oven. The evening's dinner will be served, with candles, wine and the sounds of crackling logs on the fire.

Mushroom & Turnip Pot Roast (page 61)
Quick Sautéed Kale with Cranberries
Beets with Mustard & Créme Fraîche (page 67)
Fresh baby arugula with Rosemary
Apple Walnut Vinaigrette (page 47)

ROOT VEGETABLE GRATIN

Serves 8-10

Unlike most gratins, weighed down with lots of cream and cheese, this one delivers rich flavor with just a little dairy and the sharp, nutty taste of Gruyere. It's the perfect light note in the middle of a heavy holiday meal and reheats easily for a covered dish supper.

Ingredients:

- 1 celery root, peeled
- 2 turnips, peeled
- 2 rutabagas, peeled
- 1 tbs butter
- ½ cup finely grated Parmesan cheese
- 1 cup grated Gruyere cheese
- 4 tbs chopped thyme
- 1 cup vegetable stock (page 27)
- 2-3 tbs heavy cream

Directions:

- Preheat oven to 400 degrees.
- Cut celery root, turnips and rutabagas into 2" wide chunks. With a knife or mandolin, cut into ¼" thick slices.
- Coat inside of a 9" x 9" baking dish with butter. Add 1-2 tbs grated Parmesan and turn dish to coat bottom and sides.
- Place a single layer of celery root in the bottom of dish. Sprinkle with Parmesan, Gruyere and thyme. Season with salt and pepper. Add a layer of turnips and repeat with cheeses, thyme, salt and pepper. Next, add a layer of rutabagas topped with cheeses, thyme, salt and pepper. Repeat layers until the dish is filled. Pour stock over gratin and sprinkle top with Parmesan.
- Cover tightly with foil and place in oven for 1 hour.
- Remove gratin from over and uncover. Drizzle cream over gratin and return to oven uncovered. Cook 30-45 minutes longer, until vegetables can be easily pierced with a knife.
- Remove from oven and let rest 5-10 minutes while vegetables absorb remaining liquid.

TIP: It will look like you're not adding enough liquid, but trust me. We tested this 6 times over the course of a year to get the right amount.

THE EVIL MANDOLIN

My first mandolin was a v-slicer, and the first time I used it was to remove corn from the cob for creamed-corn, a dish I was making for the first time. While effective, the kernels were leaping all over the counter. Jason, standing behind me, said "you're doing that wrong." I handed him the mandolin.

On his first pass, the blade went into the tip of his finger. Now, while most mandolin injuries aren't serious, they tend to produce a lot of blood. Jason dropped the mandolin and pulled his hand back fast enough that the corn was untainted. He's never touched a mandolin again.

Lessons learned? Always use the guard. And if you don't want to get asked to do something again, do it wrong the first time.

BEETS WITH MUSTARD & CRÈME FRAICHE

Serves 6–8

Sounds bizarre, right? Turns out mustard and crème fraîche bring out the best in beets. These rock. But no, Jason won't eat them.

Ingredients:

2 tbs butter

3 large beets, cut in a ½" dice

1 tbs chopped thyme

½ cup Sherry vinegar

¼ cup crème fraîche

1 tbs Dijon mustard

1 tbs capers

Directions:

- ‣ Melt butter in a saucepan over medium-low heat.
- ‣ Add beets, thyme and vinegar. Cover and cook until beets are soft and easily pierced with a fork, about 20-30 minutes.
- ‣ Stir in crème fraîche and mustard and toss with capers. Season to taste with salt, pepper and a splash of vinegar

CUTTING COMMENTARY

This recipe tells you to cut your beets in a ½" dice, while some recipes give you no direction at all. How big should a dice be?

First of all, they're all just guidelines. You may just be developing your knife skills, or maybe you're cooking at a friend's house with her dull knife (while sowing the seeds for regular knife sharpening—or you'll never cook there again. Seriously.). If cutting 3 beets into a ½" dice would take you 15 minutes, then cut them into 1" chunks.

What's the impact? You'll have to cook them longer, which probably means adding a little more liquid to the pan and a longer cooking time. It also means bigger pieces of beet kicking around longer in your mouth while you chew them, so you may want to add a little extra mustard and crème fraîche so there's plenty of sauce. That's it, no major crisis and the world hasn't come to an end. Remember rule #1 of cooking. Make it fun!

TIP: Crème fraiche is sour cream for grownups. You can find it in the cheese or dairy case at the grocery store. Or make your own (see sidebar page 183).

COW FOOD

"I've finally done it!" I exclaimed. "I have come up with a great rutabaga dish."

"No you haven't," replied my husband Jason. "Rutabagas are cow feed and taste terrible."

Poor rutabagas. These beautiful, purple-topped root vegetables are a country-mouse-cousin of the turnip, probably originating in the Netherlands. Rutabagas are a naturally-occurring hybrid between cabbage and the turnip (there will be a test on this later). The creamsicle orange flesh is coarse and sports the bitter, sharp taste common to many of its relatives in the mustard, or *Brassica*, family (this will also be on the test).

Each fall, covered in a daunting coating of paraffin wax, they arrive at the farm market just as autumn favorites like apples, squash and cauliflower have lost the shine of newness. And each fall I try to cook them in an interesting new way; steamed then glazed, mashed, boiled or roasted.

The results are always good, but never better. My valiant struggle to create a great rutabaga dish had failed. Until…

The inspiration I needed came with my return to live farm market cooking demos at the end of a particularly long, harsh winter. With fields too cold for spring vegetables, I grabbed what I could—root vegetables stored through the winter. Boiled with leeks, garlic and potatoes until truly tender, I passed the rutabagas through a food mill. Magically, the sharp taste had mellowed. I added sharp, nutty bleu cheese to cut through the starch and a little butter for richness. Parsley made them fresh and bright.

Thrilled with my success I plated my achievement and proudly presented it to Jason, who incidentally hates bleu cheese.

"They're like mashed potatoes, only terrible!" he cried. "Why would you do this?"

Just ignore him. They're delicious.

TIP: A food mill or ricer will keep the mashed rutabaga and potato fluffy and light. Stir in the butter and cheese while the mixture is still hot and steaming.

TIP: Rutabagas take longer to cook than potatoes, so cut the rutabagas in cubes half the size of the potato.

BLEU MASHED RUTABAGA & POTATO

Serves 8

While many would argue that mashed potatoes, on their own, are the most perfect food ever created, this pairing with creamy bleu cheese and mustardy rutabaga is pretty darn good!

Ingredients:

2 large starchy potatoes, like Russets, peeled and cut in 1" cubes

1 large rutabaga, peeled and cut in ½" cubes

3 cloves garlic, peeled

1 tbs salt

2 leeks

3 tbs butter

1 ½ cups creamy bleu cheese

¼ cup chopped parsley

⅛ tsp cardamom

Directions:

- Place potatoes, rutabaga and garlic in a stock pot with 1 tbs salt. Cover by 2" with water.

- Remove top greens from leeks (you can save them for stock). Quarter and rinse the white part. Roughly chop and add to the stock pot.

- Bring to a boil, then reduce heat and simmer for about ½ hour or until potato and rutabaga are soft.

- Strain solids, discarding the liquid. Press the potato and rutabaga mixture through the medium disc of a food mill or through a ricer, into a medium bowl.

- Stir butter and bleu cheese into warm, milled vegetables. Add parsley and cardamom.

- Season to taste with salt and pepper.

PUTTING IT TOGETHER: SHEPHERD'S PIE

Kicking off my 2014 season of cooking demonstrations at DC's historic Eastern Market, I decided to create four dishes that could be combined as layers of a shepherd's pie. Each dish tasted great served alone, but the whole was even more delicious than the sum of the parts.

Just like traditional shepherd's pie, it's a perfect way to cook creatively through the week and give new life to leftovers. Here are the layers from the top down.

Top: Bleu Mashed Rutabaga & Potato
Layer 3: Celery Root & Cheese Salad (page 75)
Layer 2: Apricot Chile Glazed Carrots (page 73)
Bottom: Ground Lamb with Mushrooms & Spinach (page 77)

APRICOT CHILE GLAZED CARROTS

Serves 6

The musky notes of apricot and earthy chile flakes ground the sweetness of the carrots and preserves. A little heat makes them pop!

Ingredients:

- 4 carrots cut in 2" matchsticks, about 4 cups
- 2 tbs butter
- 2 shallots, thinly sliced
- ⅛ tsp crushed red pepper flakes
- ½ cup apricot preserves
- 3 tbs white balsamic vinegar
- White pepper

Directions:

- Steam carrots 5–6 minutes until still very firm in center. Remove from heat and leave covered.
- Melt 2 tbs butter in 12" skillet over medium-low heat.
- Add shallots and cook until they begin to turn a rich, caramelized brown. Add pepper flakes and cook for one minute longer.
- Add carrots and a pinch of salt. Cook, stirring a few times, until carrots begin to brown on edges.
- Add apricot preserves and vinegar and toss, glazing the carrots as the preserves melt and the vinegar reduces.
- Season to taste with additional salt, white pepper and vinegar.

TIP: Steaming the carrots first means you don't have to cook them as long in the pan, allowing them to brown quickly without burning.

THANKSGIVING IN MARCH

My cousin-in-law Sarah started a wonderful tradition. Each March, she and her husband Mike gather together at my Aunt and Uncle's home, along with my cousin Laura, for Thanksgiving in March. The holiday was created so they could enjoy one of their favorite meals without a huge crowd, while trying out some non-traditional recipes. This year, home for a month to write the stories for this cookbook, I was invited.

It was a perfect day at Aunt Ali and Uncle Paul's. We relaxed, gathered together in the kitchen, casually cooking and pouring a few drinks. More than twelve hours flashed by in a pleasant blur of easy conversation and laughter. I was honored to receive a coveted seat at the table—and overjoyed to add my Root Vegetable Gratin and Apricot and Chile Glazed Carrots to a table filled with incredible food.

I'm already currying favor for next year's invitation. I've been told a pot of Celery Root Soup just may clinch the deal.

73

CELERY ROOT & CHEESE SALAD

Serves 6

Warm celery root softens young Gouda cheese providing creamy balance to a sharp vinaigrette.

For salad:

2 cups grated Gouda cheese
½ red onion, thinly sliced
½ cup chopped parsley
1 head celery root, cut
    in ¼" cubes
1 tbs salt

For dressing:

1 clove garlic, minced
⅓ cup red wine vinegar
2 tbs grainy mustard
1 tbs chopped thyme
¼ cup walnut oil
¼ cup olive oil—the good stuff!

Directions:

- In a medium bowl, toss together cheese, onion and parsley.

- Begin vinaigrette: Sprinkle minced garlic with coarse salt and mash into paste on your cutting board using the flat edge of your knife. In a small bowl, whisk together garlic paste, vinegar, mustard and thyme. Season to taste with pepper and additional salt.

- Boil water in a 4 quart saucepan. Add celery root with 1 tbs salt and cook until softened but still firm in the center.

- Remove celery root from water with a slotted spoon and toss immediately with cheese and onion mixture.

- Finish vinaigrette: While whisking, drizzle oil into vinegar mixture. This will form a creamy emulsion.

- Dress salad to taste, seasoning with salt and pepper.

TIP: This salad is best made with young Gouda, mild and creamy. Nutty and crumbly aged Gouda, however, is delicious for a cheese board.

TIP: Yes, this salad is warm. It's okay. Don't freak out. The melty cheese is totally worth stepping outside your comfort zone.

CHEESE AND A HANDSHAKE

As March closed out the winter of 2013-2014, Sona Creamery opened on Capitol Hill in Washington, DC. Owners Genevieve and Conan O'Sullivan welcomed me warmly with a handshake and a delicious selection of cheese sold by the pound which also serves as the inspiration for their café menu.

The first cheese they sent me home with was Coolea. It is made in County Cork Ireland by a family (now the second generation) who moved to Ireland from the Netherlands, quite literally in search of greener pastures. They found them and started making cheese that quickly attracted a following. Made in the Gouda style, it is sold young—tasting creamy but not as sweet.

Coolea originally inspired this recipe. While more commonly sold substitutes make it easier to repeat a recipe just about anywhere, it's no reason not to use special, locally available ingredients when you find them. That's part of the fun.

TIP: Maitake mushrooms are earthy and rich. If you can't find
them, a blend of Criminis and Shitakes will get you deliciously
close.

GROUND LAMB WITH MUSHROOMS & SPINACH

Serves 6

Oregano, rosemary and chives take pleasantly gamey lamb to a whole other bright, fresh and earthy place. Spinach keeps it light.

Ingredients:

3 tbs olive oil, divided
4 cups chopped Maitake mushrooms
1 shallot, minced
¼ cup dry white wine
Nutmeg
¼ cup chopped parsley
1 large onion, chopped
1 pound ground lamb
½ tsp ground Urfa pepper or chili powder
1 tsp lemon zest
1 tbs chopped oregano
1 tbs chopped chives
2 tbs chopped rosemary
½ pound baby spinach

Directions:

- Heat 2 tbs olive oil in 12" skillet over medium-high heat. Add mushrooms and sauté until softened and beginning to brown.

- Add minced shallot and cook until softened, about 2 minutes longer.

- Deglaze pan with wine. Season to taste with salt, pepper, nutmeg and parsley. Remove mixture from pan and reserve.

- Return pan to medium-high heat and warm remaining 1 tbs olive oil. Add chopped onion and cook until softened.

- Add ground lamb. Cook until browned. Drain fat and return pan to heat. Add cooked mushrooms and warm through.

- Mix in Urfa pepper, lemon zest, oregano, chives and rosemary. Season to taste with salt and pepper.

- Stir in baby spinach, which will lightly wilt from the hot ingredients.

GOING ON A TREASURE HUNT

Ever find a really great recipe, your mouth watering just from the ingredients list? Then bam!—an ingredient you don't know or sounds difficult to find. What's a cook to do?

Option 1: Give up. Grab a frozen dinner, and place it in the microwave. A terrible idea.

Option 2: Substitute. Head to the internet and look up the oddball or unfamiliar ingredient—say Urfa pepper. Discover this Turkish ingredient is sun-dried with a raisiny richness and, while mild, has heat that builds nicely while eating. Guajillo pepper or chile powder would substitute perfectly well. You could also just find and order the ingredient online. Definitely better than the frozen dinner.

Option 3: Search. Hit the local specialty grocer or try that spice store or ethnic market you've been meaning to visit. If you don't find what you are looking for, you may discover a great new source of ingredients, and you can always go back to Option 2.

Never pass up the adventure of a new recipe just because you can't find a new ingredient. Life's too short, and you're not building a nuclear reactor. It's just dinner.

spring

IN SEASON.
As a child, asparagus was a special sign of spring's arrival, a treat served with homemade Hollandaise or stir-fried with soy sauce and garlic. Months later, as my birthday approached in August, my Mom would ask what I wanted for dinner.

"Asparagus, please!" I would say.

"Asparagus is only available in spring," she would reply, foisting on me some freshly-picked corn on the cob, dripping in butter, and a thick slice of her lemon cake. Life was hard.

At the age of twenty-two, I lived at home for a few months in the spring. Feeding a newly discovered passion for cooking, I spent hours pouring over cookbooks and in the kitchen. I discovered that my prized asparagus was now available year 'round. It was no longer so special. My joy for fresh produce heralding spring's arrival was saved only by the discovery that wild collection preserved a magically short season for fiddlehead ferns—only 2–3 weeks each year.

At thirty, I moved to Washington, DC and fell in love—twice. My first love was Jason, who is now my husband. He brought me to Capitol Hill and introduced me to my second love, Eastern Market. Living just a few blocks

away, I began shopping there exclusively. Over the year that followed, my diet changed. Food once again became seasonal: Winter stark, spring sparse, summer bountiful and fall rich.

Most importantly, I found renewed joy in the seasonality of food. The arrival and departure of crops accompanied by changes in weather—like the blooming of flowers—ties our lives to the calendar with an almost circadian rhythm. Asparagus arrives each spring after the appearance of bitter greens, peppery radishes and the long, slow tease of winter's thaw. It's first stems, irregular and touched with purple, are sugary sweet, needing little more than light blanching, a sharp vinaigrette and the yolk running from one perfectly poached egg.

When asparagus first arrives, Jason and I joyfully eat it every night only to find, two weeks later, the newness wearing off. Growing bored, our preparations are more adventurous, simple vinaigrettes giving way to soups and sauces. Another two weeks and it's the end of the season. The stems are now tougher and more grassy, less sweet. But, whether wrapped in buttery phyllo, baked in a quiche or heavily seasoned, we eat every last stem, knowing it will be ten and a half months before fresh, crisp, sugary asparagus returns to the market.

Of course, we could buy it all year (and on a desperate day in mid-winter, we might} but nothing compares to asparagus picked fresh, locally, and eaten as soon as you can get it to the kitchen. That, like the prized asparagus of my childhood, is only available for six weeks each spring.

JONATHAN BARDZIK

TIP: You'll almost never hear me advocate for a tool that has only
one use, but an old-fashioned egg slicer just makes life so easy.
Plus, my Mom always uses one, so it makes me smile.

EGG SPINACH POTATO SALAD

Serves 6

This fresh egg salad is lightened with baby spinach and substitutes a crisp vinaigrette for heavy mayonnaise. Fingerling potatoes easily replace the richness you'll never miss.

Ingredients:

1 ½ pounds fingerling potatoes
6 eggs, hard-boiled
¼ pound baby spinach
2 tbs garlic chives, minced
½ red onion, diced, divided
2 tbs Dijon mustard
2 tbs Sherry vinegar
¼ cup plus 2 tbs olive oil—the good stuff!
1 tbs finely chopped rosemary

Directions:

- Slice fingerling potatoes into ¼" coins. Boil in lightly salted water for 10–15 minutes until tender but still firm in the center. Remove from water and drain.

- Finely chop eggs and spinach. Combine in a medium bowl with garlic chives and all but 2 tbs of red onion.

- Make vinaigrette: Whisk together reserved 2 tbs red onion, mustard and vinegar. Season with salt and pepper. While whisking, drizzle ¼ cup oil into vinegar mixture. This will form a creamy emulsion.

- Drizzle potatoes with remaining 2 tbs oil. Toss with rosemary and season to taste with salt and pepper.

- Taste spinach salad with a bit of the vinaigrette, season to taste with additional vinegar or oil.

- Lightly dress salad and serve over potatoes.

A BIG COMMITMENT

Easter eggs are like puppies and children. Cuteness and fun up front with lots of responsibility on the backside. Sure, sitting in a sunny kitchen, watching colorful tablets dissolve like Alka Seltzer in cups of vinegar and boiling water seems like the start of a magic adventure. But five days later, it's all over and you've got two dozen hard-boiled eggs taunting you every time you open the fridge.

You'll eat a couple for breakfast. Each afternoon your kids sneak back into the kitchen to quietly return the eggs you placed, lovingly, in their lunch box that morning. Enter the egg salad. No, not the mayonnaise bomb that adds more inches to your chocolate-bunny-bloated waist. This salad is light with lots of greens. A vinaigrette keeps flavors fresh and a bed of warm potatoes makes it hearty enough for a meal.

Happy day-after-Easter. I dare you not to like it. You may even start hard-boiling eggs for no reason at all.

BALSAMIC SHALLOT MARMALADE

Makes about 2 cups

What do you do with sweet, caramelized shallot marmalade? Use it everywhere—on sautéed, grilled or roasted meats, over a salad of fresh greens with a champagne vinaigrette, or tucked into your morning omelet.

Ingredients:

- 2 tbs grape seed or vegetable oil
- 1 pound shallots, thinly sliced
- ½ cup balsamic vinegar
- ⅓ cup maple or brown sugar
- Nutmeg
- Cardamom

Directions:

- Warm oil in 12" skillet over medium-high heat. Add shallots and saute.

- When shallots begin to brown, reduce heat and continue to cook until softened, about 10 minutes.

- Add vinegar, scraping bottom to release any brown bits. Stir in sugar, a pinch of nutmeg and a pinch of cardamom. Continue cooking another 5–10 minutes until thick and jammy.

- Season to taste with salt and additional nutmeg and cardamom.

TIP: Watch the shallots carefully. Once they begin to break down and most of their liquid evaporates, turn down the heat to avoid burning.

WHAT'S A SHALLOT?

A shallot looks like a small onion. Depending on the variety, they can be short, squat and gold or long and red. It's what an onion wants to be when it grows up.

My Dad asked me recently, "What does that mean?"

"Dad," I said, "I know you've had a few glasses of gin." (That's throughout his life, not just that night.) "I know you've had some Beefeater which has a strong juniper berry flavor to it and I know you've also had Bombay Sapphire which is clean and smooth. Well, shallots are the Bombay Sapphire of the onion world."

And I poured us each another drink.

ASPARAGUS WITH PISTACHIO CREAM SAUCE

Serves 4

This is a surprisingly light yet complex sauce with well-balanced flavors. Ten minutes of infusing will give you a perfect pairing for asparagus. Twenty minutes will bring out more bay and cardamom, magical with fresh cauliflower in the fall or baked white fish.

Ingredients:

½ cup shelled pistachios, rinsed if salted

2 bay leaves

½ cup thinly sliced shallot

3 whole cardamom pods or ⅛ tsp ground

¼ tsp whole black peppercorns

2 cups cream

1 tbs Sherry vinegar

1 bunch asparagus, about 1 pound

Directions:

- Mix together pistachios, bay leaves, shallot, cardamom, peppercorns and cream in a small saucepan.

- Bring to a simmer and cook for 10 minutes.

- Strain mixture, reserving solids. Return cream to saucepan.

- Add vinegar to cream and simmer until slightly thickened, about 3 minutes. Season to taste with salt, pepper and additional vinegar.

- Meanwhile, simmer asparagus in a pan of salted water until crisp tender.

- Serve asparagus topped with cream sauce and reserved shallots and pistachios.

PUTTING IT TOGETHER: DAFFODILS & OPEN WINDOWS

Though the appearance of crocus comes with the risk of one more snowfall, bright yellow daffodils and crisp, fresh breezes through open windows are the first signs that spring has truly arrived. It's a night to eat in your kitchen, sucking the juice of tender lamb from your fingers, greedily eating the first sugary stalks of fresh asparagus and toasting, over candlelight, the start of another year in the garden.

Sorrel Soup (page 93)
Herb and Cornmeal Crusted
Rack of Lamb (page 95)
Asparagus with Pistachio Cream Sauce

TIP: If your pistachios come heavily salted, rinse them under water so they don't throw off the flavor of your sauce.

STRAWBERRY RHUBARB SHRUB

Makes 3-4 cups syrup

There are so many ways to use this tart syrup. I like a ratio of 3 tbs to ½ cup sparkling water for a light, refreshing drink. Or try muddling some mint and mix the shrub with rum or vodka and a splash of bitters. You just made your new favorite spring drink!

Ingredients:

1 cup sugar
1 cup water
4 cups strawberries, hulled and halved
4 cups chopped rhubarb stalks, cut in 1" pieces
½ tsp black peppercorns
Vinegar—this is the fun part! (See tip)

Directions:

- Mix sugar and water in a 3 quart saucepan over medium-high heat. Bring to a simmer and stir until sugar is dissolved.

- Add rhubarb stalks, strawberries and peppercorns. Stir occasionally as fruit releases liquid and returns to a simmer. Cook for 15 minutes. Cool and strain through a sieve, pressing on solids to release liquid.

- Mix 4 parts fruit syrup to 1 part vinegar. Store in the refrigerator.

WHAT IS A SHRUB?

Having absolutely nothing to do with the landscaping in front of your house, a shrub is an American adaptation of a British method for preserving fruit. It consists of fruit mixed with vinegar and left to macerate anywhere from a day to several weeks. The solid fruit is strained leaving a tart liquid that is sweetened with sugar and reduced to a syrup that can be sipped on its own or added to other beverages. They not only tasted good, but made important nutrients available through long winters.

Though they fell out of favor with the widespread availability of home refrigeration in the 1930's, the craft cocktail movement has rediscovered them. One sip and you'll wonder why they ever went away.

TIP: From balsamic and red wine to the many fruit infused vinegars in my pantry, I couldn't find a vinegar I didn't like! Experiment and have fun!

AN INVITATION

In May of 2002, I received a charming invitation.

"You are a fabulous cook," my friend Peter said. "Our friend Gordon is a wine expert and has a beautiful home. Therefore, it seems to me that if I buy the ingredients and the wines that Gordon recommends, and you cook dinner at his house, we would have a wonderful evening." How could I say no?

Doubting Peter's generous assessment of my early culinary skills, I poured over stacks of cookbooks. And, brashly ignoring advice I disregard to this day, I built a menu almost entirely of dishes I had never made before. I selected tart, sorrel soup, richly balanced with butter to start the meal. For our main plate, the crossed, Frenched bones of a cornmeal crusted rack of lamb would stand above asparagus roasted with balsamic vinegar, alongside a rosemary potato galette. A Bavarian Cream—vanilla custard thickened with gelatin and lightened with whipped cream—would provide an elegant finish.

On the night of the dinner, Peter, his boyfriend Eric, and I arrived at Gordon's home. We quickly settled into wine and conversation that was as stimulating as it was easy. In the midst of my preparations to ready the lamb for roasting, Gordon dramatically announced that his recommended wine pairings had underestimated the quality of my cooking. Ducking into his cellar, he returned with a bottle of Bordeaux.

Our evening was truly magical. Gordon (who it turns out is one of the top American experts on Bordeaux) brilliantly took us through tasting a wine he revealed was worth about $800 per bottle. Despite my having barely enough culinary knowledge to be dangerous, the meal was a success—the lamb rare, the potatoes crisply crusted, tender inside, and only a couple of lumps in the custard which turned out beautifully from its fluted mold.

However, it was not the exceptional wine, the food, or the elegant home that made the night truly special. It was the four of us, coming together. With a little planning, a little work, and a little care we elevated that night's dinner into one of the most memorable meals of my life.

So take a chance. Bust out a recipe you've never tried before, lay out your good dishes, and invite someone special to join you. You never know, your next meal might just be one you will never forget.

TIP: Cooked sorrel turns a dull olive green and there is nothing
    you can do about it except enjoy your bowl of delicious soup
    and tell your guests that it's supposed to look exactly the
    way it does.

SORREL SOUP

Serves 6

Sorrel is a beautiful, tart, lemony, leafy green, balanced in this soup by rich chicken stock and fresh butter. Make it with the first spring leaves for a delicate start to an elegant meal or just a Tuesday night supper served with salad and a crusty, toothy loaf of bread.

Ingredients:

¼ pound butter

1 large yellow onion, diced

1 clove garlic, minced

2 red potatoes, diced

2 pounds sorrel, de-ribbed and chopped

6 cups chicken stock (page 29)

2 sprigs thyme

2 bay leaves

2 tbs minced parsley

Sherry vinegar

Nutmeg

Crème fraîche (optional)

Directions:

- Melt butter in 6 quart soup pot over medium heat. Add onion, garlic and potatoes. Cook until soft. If the bottom of the pan gets dry, add water as needed.

- Add sorrel and cook for additional 8–10 minutes. As sorrel cooks, it will turn a dull, olive green.

- Add chicken stock, thyme springs and bay leaves. Simmer for 20 minutes longer.

- Remove thyme sprigs and bay leaves. Purée soup with food mill or immersion blender.

- Season to taste with a splash of vinegar, salt, pepper, a pinch of nutmeg and a tablespoon or two of additional butter. Serve topped with a generous dollop of crème fraîche.

SEEKING SORREL

I was lured in by flowery language. Sorrel soup, the recipe read, was a classic, elegant and delicate harbinger of spring, creamy and tart, like watercress—the soup you imagine served at a ladies luncheon in delicate china bowls, delivering portions far too small to possibly satisfy. I not only wanted to make this soup, I was ready to go buy a set of dishes for it.

But there's a hitch. Sorrel can be difficult to track down, often only found in the grocery store packaged in a plastic case, a few overpriced leaves at a time, with the other fresh herbs. If you're lucky, you'll find it fresh by the pound at your farm market or specialty grocer. If not, this is God's way of encouraging you to plant some seeds in your garden at home. Make sure to plant them at the far end, near the rhubarb, so you don't till them under when you turn your soil in the spring.

HERB & CORNMEAL CRUSTED RACK OF LAMB

Serves 4

Nothing says "spring has arrived" quite so elegantly as a rack of lamb, with Frenched bones crisscrossed above a plate of asparagus and young potatoes. The herbed cornmeal crust balances the pleasantly gamey flavor of the meat.

Ingredients:

- 2 cloves of garlic, minced
- 2 tbs grainy mustard
- ¼ cup chopped mixed herbs including rosemary, parsley, chives, mint
- ¼ cup cornmeal
- 2 tbs Porcini olive oil or any good olive oil from your cupboard
- 2 tbs vegetable oil
- 8 rib rack of lamb, Frenched and cut in half

Directions:

- Sprinkle minced garlic with coarse salt and mash into a paste on your cutting board using the flat edge of your knife. Mix together in a small bowl with mustard, herbs, cornmeal and Porcini olive oil. Season with salt and pepper.

- Heat oven to 400 degrees.

- Warm vegetable oil in a heavy skillet over medium-high heat. Season lamb with salt and pepper. Sear on all sides, about 2 minutes per side.

- Let lamb rest until cool enough to touch. Spread crust mixture over the surface of the meat.

- Place lamb in a roasting pan and cook in the oven for about 20 minutes, or to 125 degrees.

- Turn oven up to 500 degrees and cook 2–3 minutes longer to brown crust. Remove from oven and let rest for 10 minutes, tented with foil.

- Carve lamb between ribs to serve.

TIP: The crust may fall off when you carve the lamb. Just lay it back over the meat when you serve it.

GETTING IT RIGHT: PREPARING YOUR LAMB FOR ROASTING

When you buy your rack of lamb, ask your butcher to "French" the bones. This means carving away the meat and fat from the ribs to leave them exposed for a classic presentation. You can also ask them to crack the bones between the ribs, making the rack easier to carve when it comes out of the oven.

Your rack of lamb will likely come with a translucent, silver skin over the meat. This will get tough and gristly while cooking, ruining the experience of biting into tender, medium-rare, pleasantly gamey meat. Steel yourself for it, like the small, hard brown divots covering your pineapple, there's no way to remove this skin without sacrificing meat, but it's well worth it. The layer of fat below can be left intact, lightly scored to better hold the crust. To leave as much meat as possible, make sure you are working with a sharp knife. And it's perfectly alright if you need a shot of whiskey to steady your hands.

TIP: Many root vegetables turn brown when peeled, requiring a dunk in water mixed with vinegar or lemon juice to keep their color. Celery root holds up just fine in this recipe so don't bother with the extra step.

CELERY ROOT SLAW WITH POPPY SEED DRESSING

Serves 8

Celery root, the ugliest vegetable in the world, reveals delicious, creamy white flesh when peeled. Eaten raw it delivers a light celery taste. It's enhanced by this earthy, honey-sweetened dressing thickened with grated onion rather than rich mayonnaise.

For dressing:

- 3 tbs finely grated onion
- ½ tsp dry mustard
- ½ tsp sweet Hungarian paprika
- 1 tsp poppy seeds
- 2 tbs honey
- ¼ cup Sherry vinegar
- ½ cup vegetable or other neutral flavored oil, like grape seed

For salad:

- 4 cups grated celery root
- 2-3 tbs chopped fennel fronds or tarragon

Directions:

- Begin dressing: Whisk together onion, mustard, paprika, poppy seeds, honey, vinegar and a pinch of salt and pepper. Set aside.
- Toss together celery root and fennel fronds or tarragon in a medium bowl.
- Finish dressing: While whisking, drizzle oil into vinegar mixture. This will form a creamy emulsion.
- Season to taste with salt and pepper. Adjust vinegar and honey to achieve desired balance of sweetness and acidity.
- Toss salad with ¾ of the dressing to start. Add more to taste. The celery root is distinct, but mild, and you don't want to cover up the flavor. Let rest for thirty minutes before serving.

PUTTING IT TOGETHER: CELEBRATING MOM

For forty years, my family owned a garden center. Each of those years, my Mom spent Mother's Day working at the store, helping hapless husbands (often with children in tow) select the perfect hanging baskets and potted azaleas for their own wives and mothers. Each year she would come home tired, and each year, we would "surprise" her with a special dinner to celebrate how amazing she was (and still is) because she had spent Mother's Day, like every other day of the year, bringing joy to others—finding her joy in the smiles on their faces.

Asparagus Soup with
Mushroom Spaetzle (pages 109 & 111)
Honey & Chive Glazed Pork (page 123)
Celery Root Slaw with Poppy Seed Dressing
Rhubarb Curd with Fresh Berries
(page 101)

TIP: When you start whisking the peanut butter into the peanut sauce it will appear to "break" and look
shredded. Give it time and it will come together into a smooth, velvety sauce.

TIP: This is not the time to use baby spinach, which will "melt" while stir-frying. Use spinach with a little
more substance.

POTATOES WITH PEANUT SAUCE & GARLIC SPINACH

Serves 6

Hearty but not heavy, garlic-y, barely-wilted spinach lightens a rich peanut sauce brightened by hot chile oil and the mild, fresh acidity of rice wine vinegar. Using low starch potatoes like baby reds or fingerlings, keeps the dish from getting gummy.

Ingredients:

- 2 pounds baby red potatoes
- ¼ cup smooth peanut butter, natural tastes best
- 1 tbs hot chile oil
- 2 tbs toasted sesame oil, divided
- 6 tbs Tamari soy sauce, divided
- 3 tbs rice wine vinegar, divided
- ¼ cup warm water
- 4 tbs vegetable oil, divided
- 1" ginger, peeled and minced
- 4 cloves of garlic, minced and divided
- ½ pound field spinach
- 1 tbs sesame seeds, toasted

Directions:

- Boil potatoes in salted water until you can just pierce the center with the tip of a knife. Drain and halve when cool.

- Whisk together peanut butter, hot chile oil, 1 tbs sesame oil, 4 tbs soy sauce, 2 tbs rice wine vinegar and warm water.

- Heat 2 tbs vegetable oil in a 12" skillet over medium-high heat. Add potatoes and cook until beginning to brown. Add ginger and half of the minced garlic. Cook 1 minute and remove from heat. Toss potatoes in bowl with peanut sauce.

- Whisk together 1 tbs sesame oil, 2 tbs soy and 1 tbs rice wine vinegar into a sauce for the spinach.

- Warm remaining 2 tbs vegetable oil in clean 12" skillet over medium-high heat. Add remaining garlic and cook 30 seconds.

- Add spinach, turning in the pan just until bright green. Remove spinach and dress with sauce and sesame seeds. Top with potatoes.

SOUNDS WEIRD, TASTES GREAT

No, peanut sauce is probably not the first flavor pairing that comes to mind for potatoes. It's actually the 17th thing that came to my mind—after the 16 other potato recipes I developed.

In the test kitchen, we face challenges from early spring's sparse availability to the long-running summer and fall seasons when we are faced with the same ingredients week after week. Trust me, coming up with new recipes for tomatoes and zucchini for eight to twelve weeks in a row inspires great creativity and some strange ideas.

From fried eggplant with peaches to a warm strawberry soup, they have all been surprisingly successful (except savory stir-fried rhubarb, about which we will never speak again). Get in the kitchen and take a chance. After all, it's just dinner.

RHUBARB CURD

Makes 2 ½ to 3 cups

Like lemon curd, this recipe flavored with rhubarb syrup is a decadently rich, sweet-tart confection. It's beautiful served under fresh spring berries and is just begging to be baked into a batch of rhubarb squares.

Ingredients:

6-8 stalks rhubarb, cut in 1" pieces
¾ cup sugar, divided
4 eggs
1 tbs white balsamic vinegar
1 tsp lemon juice
4 tbs butter, chilled

Directions:

- Place rhubarb and ¼ cup sugar in 1 small saucepan. Cover rhubarb with 1" water and simmer for 20 minutes. Strain, pressing solids to remove liquid. Discard solids and reserve rhubarb juice.
- Lightly beat eggs in a small saucepan. Whisk in ⅔ cup rhubarb juice, vinegar and remaining ½ cup sugar.
- Place over medium-low heat. Stirring constantly with a wooden spoon, cook until the custard thickens and coats the back of the spoon.
- Remove from heat and whisk in butter. Press through a strainer to remove any lumps. Season to taste with lemon juice to achieve desired tartness.
- Chill sauce until thickened and use within 1 week.

TIP: The rich flavor and deep, golden color of the egg yolks will overpower the tart flavor and bright pink color of the rhubarb juice. The vinegar and lemon juice keep the flavor of the rhubarb from getting lost.

TIP: What does "coats the back of a wooden spoon" mean? Your custard is done when you pull the spoon out from stirring, draw your finger down through the custard on the spoon, and it leaves a clean trail rather than running back together.

CUSTARD JUST CAN'T TAKE THE HEAT

The first egg custard I made was a zabaglione, a whisked custard. What I didn't know then was that slow heat allows the tightly spiruled proteins in egg yolk to unfurl in long strands, then catch together forming a gel that delivers custard's smooth texture. And that's why that didn't happen that night. My zabaglione, cooked over too high a temperature, quickly turned into a bowl of sugary, boozy, scrambled eggs, (nearly) unfit for consumption.

The key to rhubarb curd is to keep the heat low and stir constantly, making sure you get your spoon into the "corners" of the pan. Once the custard thickens, whisking in cold butter stops the cooking process. Straining it through a fine mesh sieve removes the inevitable bits of scrambled egg.

A SINGLE MAN & HIS LONELY DINNER

It's sad but true.

Men, left on their own, are doomed to a life of helpless bachelorhood. Socks go un-darned, baseboards un-dusted and, worst of all, the kitchen completely unused. Just watch any Hungry-Man frozen dinner ad, and you'll see some sad sack in a flannel shirt rescued from starvation by the modern miracle of reheatable foil pans of food. Something with a congealed brown sauce.

With the exception of my brother, who reheats frozen dinners just to spite me*, the reality is that I see more and more men (and young women) discovering the joys of their kitchens. Unfettered from a burdensome expectation to put three solid meals a day on the table, men find cooking liberating—a creative outlet with a great sense of accomplishment. I'm sure that mothers and wives everywhere bite their lips and offer encouragement, hoping that laundry might be man's next domestic frontier.

Recently, feeling particularly manly, I busted out a bunch of asparagus. No delicate sauces, runny poached eggs or sharp, hand-whisked vinaigrettes for me. I was making a stick-to-your-ribs, hearty meal.

With sautéed steak tips putting the red in my meat, I wanted something earthy to ground the rich beef and sweet, crisp veggies. Eyeing portabellas, I wondered if they would be too meaty, too bold for the early spring asparagus. The pairing, it turns out, was perfectly balanced. A rich sauce—Béarnaise—with the fresh taste of tarragon, pulled the plate together.

The final result was hearty enough for any hungry man. And it will make his Mom proud, too.

*Alec, sorry for throwing you under the bus for a cheap laugh. I know you can boil pasta, too.

TIP: Crowding the mushrooms or the steak in your skillet will result in the release of a lot of liquid which means, whether you want to or not, you're now braising, not browning your steak and mushrooms. Make sure your pan is hot and cook those ingredients in multiple batches if needed.

SIRLOIN, ASPARAGUS & PORTABELLA WITH BÉARNAISE

Serves 6–8

Rich, meaty mushrooms and seared sirloin pair with grassy spring asparagus and sweet, buttery, tarragon-infused Béarnaise sauce for a hearty meal satisfying enough for a lumberjack and elegant enough for your wedding china.

Ingredients:

4 tbs olive oil, divided
1 pound asparagus, cut in 2" pieces
2 pounds top sirloin, cut in 1 ½" cubes
2 portabella mushroom caps, thinly sliced
2 cloves garlic, minced
¼ cup Cognac
½ cup chicken or vegetable stock (pages 29 and 27)
1 tbs red wine vinegar
1 tbs cold butter
2 tbs parsley
1 recipe Béarnaise sauce, warm (page 107)

Directions:

‣ Warm 1 tbs oil in a 12" skillet over medium-high heat. Add asparagus and cook 2 minutes. Remove from pan.

‣ Return pan to heat with 1 tbs olive oil. Season sirloin with salt and pepper. Add meat to pan in a single layer, cooking in multiple batches, if needed. Brown on all sides, about 4–5 minutes per batch. Remove from pan and reserve.

‣ Return pan to heat with remaining 2 tbs oil. Add mushrooms, cooking until browned on edges. If brown bits on bottom of pan begin to darken, reduce heat to medium. Add garlic and cook 1 minute longer. Remove and reserve.

‣ Return pan to medium-high heat. Add Cognac and deglaze, scraping up brown bits. Add stock and cook until reduced to ¼ cup. Remove from heat and whisk in cold butter. Season to taste with salt, pepper and vinegar.

‣ Toss pan sauce with reserved asparagus, sirloin and mushrooms. Serve mixture topped with parsley and Béarnaise sauce.

NON-STICK OR NOT NON-STICK?

Halfway through preparing most dishes at my live demonstrations, I can feel the anxiety. At least one person in the crowd can see the brown bits coating the bottom of the pan and they are imagining the mess I'll have to scrub out later. "If only," they think, "he had used non-stick."

I actually prefer not to. See, when you are sautéing ingredients, you actually want those brown bits that cook to the bottom of the pan. It's caramelization—which is full, delicious flavor. You just don't get as much with a non-stick pan. As for the mess, it's all going to come right off when we deglaze the pan. That means adding liquid—preferably something with some flavor like stock, wine or spirits—and scraping up the brown bits while it bubbles away. That both cleans your pan and creates a delicious pan sauce for your dish.

HOLLANDAISE SAUCE

Makes about 1 ½ cups

This classic hot egg yolk sauce is synonymous with spring asparagus and Eggs Benedict. Lemony Hollandaise has few ingredients and a delicate flavor, so break out the good butter and take the extra time to clarify it.

Ingredients:

½ pound butter
3 tbs cold water
3 egg yolks
2 tbs fresh-squeezed lemon juice
White pepper

Directions:

- Clarify butter: Melt butter in a small saucepan. Once melted, let it simmer, cooking off the water. Foam will rise to the surface. When no more foam is rising, remove the butter from the heat. Skim off the foam with a spoon and drain the butter through a cheesecloth-lined mesh sieve. Return to a clean pan and keep warm over low heat.

- Combine egg yolks and cold water in a 2 quart saucepan. Whisk for 30–40 seconds until light and frothy.

- Place over medium heat and continue whisking until tripled in volume and streaks appear in the bottom of the pan. Cook five seconds longer and remove from heat, whisking an additional 30 seconds to cool.

- Drizzle the warm clarified butter into the sauce, while whisking, to form a thick sauce.

- Whisk in lemon juice, adding just enough to balance the rich egg yolks and butterfat.

- Season to taste with salt and pepper.

TIP: If the eggs begin to look scrambled, immediately remove the pan from heat and whisk vigorously to cool.

TIP: Clarified butter produces a cleaner, more delicate flavor for the Hollandaise sauce, while melted butter adds the full flavor of milk solids to the Béarnaise sauce.

BÉARNAISE SAUCE

Makes about 1 ½ cups sauce

Does this look familiar? Béarnaise is essentially Hollandaise flavored with an herb, wine and vinegar reduction, instead of lemon juice. Your steak has never tasted so good!

Ingredients:

¼ cup dry white wine

¼ cup Champagne vinegar

1 bay leaf

½ tsp whole black peppercorns, crushed
  with the bottom of a saucepan

4 tbs chopped tarragon, divided

3 tbs cold water

3 egg yolks

1 tbs cold butter

½ cup melted butter

White pepper

Directions:

- In a small saucepan, combine wine, vinegar, bay leaf, peppercorns and 2 tbs tarragon. Simmer until reduced to about 2 tbs. Strain, discarding solids, and cool.

- Combine egg yolks and cold water in a 2 quart saucepan. If using the same saucepan from the wine reduction, allow it to cool first. Whisk for 30-40 seconds until light and frothy.

- Place pan over medium heat and continue whisking until egg yolks triple in volume and streaks appear in the bottom of the pan. Cook five seconds longer then remove from heat. Add cold butter and whisk an additional 30 seconds until melted.

- Drizzle the melted butter into the pan, while whisking, to form a thick sauce.

- Whisk in reserved wine and vinegar reduction, adding just enough to balance the rich egg yolks and butterfat.

- Season to taste with salt, pepper and remaining two tablespoons of chopped tarragon.

WHY IS HOLLANDAISE SO HARD? (SPOILER: IT'S NOT)

Hollandaise and Béarnaise are double emulsions. You start by suspending air and water in the rich fat of egg yolks then create a double emulsion with butter.

What does that all mean? An emulsion simply forces two or more liquids that don't particularly like each other to hang out for a bit. In this case, the egg yolk surrounds water and air, and then butter. The egg yolks can only handle so much liquid before the emulsion breaks.

If your sauce turns grainy while you are adding melted butter, stop whisking and strain it through a fine sieve. In a separate bowl, whisk together another egg yolk with 1 tbs cold water. While whisking, slowly add your broken sauce. Et voilà! The sauce is saved!

ASPARAGUS SOUP

Serves 6

This soup keeps delicious spring asparagus center stage, delivering a texture that is thick and rich without adding any cream to dull the fresh, sweet flavor. Garnishing a bowl with mushroom spaetzle makes it dinner party fabulous!

Ingredients:

2 bunches asparagus, about 2 pounds

2 sprigs thyme

1 bay leaf

2 tbs chopped parsley, plus stems

6 cups chicken or vegetable stock (pages 29 and 27)

4 tbs butter

2 medium red potatoes, diced

2 leeks, white and light green parts thinly sliced

Sherry vinegar

Directions:

‣ Snap tough ends from asparagus. Add ends to a 4 quart saucepan with stock, thyme springs, bay leaf and parsley stems. Simmer for 20 minutes.

‣ Melt 2 tbs butter in a soup pot over medium-low heat and add potatoes and leeks. Add a little water when pan gets dry. Cook until potatoes are tender and can be mashed easily with a fork.

‣ Strain stock, add to soup pot and cook for five minutes.

‣ Cut tender ends of asparagus into 2" pieces and add to stock. Remove 10–12 tips after 3 minutes for garnish.

‣ When asparagus is just tender, pass soup through a food mill or processor.

‣ Stir through chopped parsley and season to taste with salt, pepper, additional butter and a splash of vinegar. Garnish with asparagus tips.

TIP: Spring asparagus has a delicate, sweet flavor that is easily dulled by heavy thickeners like cream and flour. Use red potatoes, relatively low in starch, to thicken the soup letting the fresh flavor shine through.

JASON SAYS I HATE TECHNOLOGY

Actually, my husband is wrong. I love technology. But he can't imagine any other reason why I would pull a food mill from the shelf rather than sticking the business end of an electric immersion blender into a pot of asparagus soup.

The reason is that food mills leave behind the tough and fibrous parts of vegetables like apple peels, tomato skins or the tough fibers in asparagus. An immersion blender or food processor just cuts those long, tough fibers down into short, tough fibers, which still have a coarse mouthfeel. The food mill will deliver a silky, smooth purée for the best asparagus soup you've ever tasted. Well worth a bit of manual labor.

MUSHROOM SPAETZLE

Serves 6–8

These small soup dumplings deliver rich mushroom-y flavor. They are delicious tossed in butter, beautiful garnishing a bowl of asparagus soup and would pair perfectly with a thick slice of slow cooked pot roast.

Ingredients:

- 2 tbs olive oil
- 2 cups chopped Crimini mushrooms
- ¼ cup Madeira wine
- 3 tbs minced chives
- 1 ½ cups flour
- ¾ tsp salt
- 2 eggs
- ½ cup whole milk
- 3 tbs grated Parmesan cheese
- 2 tbs butter

Directions:

- Warm oil in a large skillet over medium heat.
- Add mushrooms and cook until softened and golden on edges.
- Deglaze pan with wine and scrape up any brown bits. Cook until liquid has evaporated. Season to taste with salt and pepper.
- Chop cooked mushrooms together with the chives until very finely minced.
- Bring a large pot of water to a simmer. Season generously with salt.
- Meanwhile, whisk together flour and salt. Add mushrooms and whisk to combine.
- In a separate bowl, whisk together eggs and milk. Add to dry ingredients and stir until it forms into a smooth dough.
- Press dough through a spaetzle maker or metal colander over boiling water. Cook for 2–3 minutes and remove with a slotted spoon, draining in a colander or strainer.
- Toss with parmesan and butter.

TIP: No spaetzle maker? You can use a metal colander. Set it over the water with a baseball-sized piece of dough and press it through the holes using a broad flat spoon.

GILDING THE LILY

In all honesty, a perfect bowl of creamy, sweet, spring asparagus soup does not really need a garnish. You could just stand over the stove and eat it right out of the pot, while ripping hunks off a baguette to slather with farm-fresh butter. Unfortunately your in-laws, your hot new boyfriend, or the local garden club may find this behavior a bit coarse.

Sometimes eating is just a celebration of good food. But when you are claiming an evening to honor the company of family and dear friends then set the table, lay out the fine china, iron your linens, and add a garnish to a bowl of absolutely perfect asparagus soup. May I recommend some mushroom spaetzle?

ASPARAGUS MIMOSA SALAD

Serves 4

A sharp, Champagne vinaigrette over sweet, fresh, spring asparagus with rich, grated, hard-boiled egg and peppery, crisp radish matchsticks may combine to create the most perfect salad ever. The recipe title refers to the close resemblance between grated whole eggs and the delicate, foamy flowers of the Mimosa tree.

For salad:

- 2 eggs, hard-boiled
- 1 pound asparagus
- 2–3 radishes, cut in matchsticks

For dressing:

- 1 shallot, minced
- ¼ cup Champagne vinegar
- ½ tsp Dijon mustard
- ¾ cup olive oil—the good stuff!

Directions:

- Start vinaigrette: Whisk together shallot, vinegar, mustard and a pinch of salt and pepper. Set aside.

- Peel and finely grate the hard-boiled eggs on the smallest side of a box grater. Set aside.

- Blanch asparagus in a large boiling pot of salted water for approximately 2 minutes, until crisp tender. Shock in an ice bath.

- Finish vinaigrette: While whisking, drizzle oil into vinegar mixture. This will form a creamy emulsion.

- Taste vinaigrette with an asparagus stalk and season to taste with additional salt, pepper, oil or vinegar.

- Place asparagus stalks on individual plates, drizzle with vinaigrette, top with radish and egg.

PUTTING IT TOGETHER: SEERSUCKER BRUNCH

Spring Sundays are the perfect excuse to open up the closet, slip into pastels that have lain hidden at the back for months, and partake in the world's most decadent meal—brunch. Lazily enjoyed between Saturday chores and the start of the week ahead, there's simply no better way to share a moment, and some Champagne, with friends.

Scrambled Eggs with Pea Tendrils (page 119)
Pasta Primavera (page 137)
Asparagus Mimosa Salad
Strawberry Rhubarb Shrub with sparkling water or Prosecco (page 89)

TIP: While farm fresh eggs are a delicious treat scrambled or fried, they are impossible to peel when hard-boiled. Use eggs that are a week or two old for hard boiling.

AMERICAN GINGER. American Ginger has a beautiful flower. Its diminutive, deep cup opens into three red-brown petals ending in pointed tips. Appearing below the low canopy of leaves that emerge from bare ground in early spring, the flowers bloom mere inches from the soil. Unless good fortune presents the opportunity to hold a pot at eye level in your local garden center, witnessing this beauty requires dirtying your hands and knees on the cold, muddy ground.

Only a few weeks later in the season, this subtle beauty would be lost amidst the crowded riot of summer blooms competing for our attention. In spring, we observe subtlety—we marvel at the shapes of swelling buds,

we celebrate nearly-yellow, newly unfurled leaves and their maturation to various shades of blue-green. With nearly the same attention paid to March Madness, we follow the progress of perennials pushing through barren soil, stems and leaves renewing from memory stored in their roots, underground, through the cold of winter.

Spring in the vegetable garden and in our kitchens is no different. After a winter of cellared root vegetables and preserved sugars, our taste buds leap at the first peppery radishes and tender greens. Our eyes brighten at the delicate sweetness of pea tendrils, just as our smiles will stretch broadly savoring the flavor of saccharine cherries and peaches a few warm months later.

Now, before they grow fat and lazy amidst the onslaught of summer's bounty, our taste buds are still sensitive, alert to the subtle, green flavor of fiddleheads tossed in spring butter, its sweetness tempered by the season's first herbs and flowers eaten greedily by the cows in the pasture.

In this moment of heightened awareness, celebrate bitterness and grassiness; celebrate the challenge of spring in the kitchen. Luxurious summer will be here soon enough.

JONATHAN BARDZIK

115

TIP: Ancho chiles are dried Poblanos. Their flavor is sweet and smoky, reminiscent of raisins, with mild to medium heat. The flavor is a perfect pairing with this dish. Look for the powdered version in the spice aisle or order it online. If you can't find it use some chile powder.

FIDDLEHEAD TACOS

Serves 6

When we first tested this dish, my team couldn't believe there was no meat. Neither could my audience at the farm market that weekend. Enjoy them while they last—fiddleheads are only available for a few weeks each spring.

For salsa:

- 1 bunch cilantro, finely chopped
- 2 cloves garlic, minced
- ½ red onion finely diced
- 1 tbs Sherry vinegar
- 1 tbs olive oil—the good stuff
- ½ tsp chile powder, I like Ancho for this dish
- ¼ tsp cumin

For tacos:

- ½ pound fiddlehead ferns
- 2 tbs olive oil
- 2 cloves garlic, minced
- 2 portabella mushroom caps
- ½ tsp cumin
- 1 tsp Ancho chile powder
- Red wine vinegar
- 1 cup crumbled queso fresco

Directions:

- Stir together salsa ingredients and let rest while flavors blend.
- Bring a 3 quart pot of salted water to a boil.
- Meanwhile, heat 2 tbs olive oil in a 12" skillet. Add garlic and cook 30 seconds until fragrant. Add mushrooms to pan.
- Add fiddleheads to the pot of boiling water and cook for 4 minutes. Remove fiddleheads from water with a slotted spoon, and transfer to pan with mushrooms. Continue to cook until mushrooms are softened and the edges begin to brown.
- Remove from heat. Toss mushrooms and fiddleheads with cumin and ancho chile powder. Season to taste with salt, pepper and red wine vinegar.
- Just before serving, season salsa to taste with salt, pepper and additional Sherry vinegar.
- Serve fiddleheads and mushrooms in warm, flour tortillas topped with queso fresco and salsa.

FIDDLEHEADS ARE (MOSTLY) NOT POISONOUS

Occasional cases of food poisoning have been connected to fiddlehead ferns, but the reasons are not clear. While some ferns are toxic, the Ostrich fern, Matteuchia struthiopteris (you just said it five times fast, didn't you?) is only mildly so, if at all.

Rinsing the brown skins from the fiddleheads under running water is part of playing it safe. The other half of the solution is boiling the fiddleheads before finishing them in the sauté pan. You may see recommendations for boiling them for as long as 15 minutes which will absolutely ruin this beautiful vegetable. If you make mayonnaise with raw egg yolks, you've probably got the risk tolerance for fiddleheads. The decision is yours.

SCRAMBLED EGGS WITH PEA TENDRILS

Serves 4

There are five ingredients in this dish and each one counts. Tender pea tendrils, the young shoots of pea plants, are a sweet addition to farm fresh eggs, cream and rich butter. Buy a cheddar cheese with a little bite to give the eggs a little pop.

Ingredients:

6 large eggs

3 tsp cream

2 tbs butter

1 cup pea tendrils, tough stems removed

Freshly grated cheddar cheese

Directions:

- Whisk eggs for 20–30 seconds with cream and a pinch each of salt and pepper.

- Warm a large, non-stick sauté pan over medium-low heat. Add butter to pan.

- When butter stops foaming, add eggs.

- Fold eggs gently toward middle of skillet with a rubber spatula to form large soft curds. Remove from pan when eggs are cooked, but still glistening.

- Fold in pea tendrils.

- Season to taste with salt and pepper and top with freshly grated cheese.

THE GREAT SCRAMBLED EGG DEBATE

Everyone has an opinion and a method for cooking the perfect scrambled eggs. Hot and fast or low and slow—large, firm, fluffy curds or smaller, softer and wet. It's all about preference. I prefer my curds large, but delicate in texture, tender and moist.

To achieve that, cook your eggs over medium-low heat. Stir them with a rubber spatula using broad strokes, folding the eggs gently toward the middle of the skillet. Remove them from the pan while still glistening and just a bit wet. They will continue to set off the heat.

TIP: Pick the leaves and tender tips from the pea shoots. You're not cooking them long enough to soften tough stems.

MINTED GARLIC SCAPE POTATO SALAD

Serves 4–6

Fresh mint, a sharp bright vinaigrette, and the bold, sweet garlicy flavor of the scapes make this the perfect light tasting potato salad. Perfect with roast lamb or chicken!

For salad:

- 4 cups small potatoes
- 3 tbs chopped mint
- ¼ cup finely chopped garlic scapes

For dressing:

- 1 clove garlic, minced
- ¼ cup Champagne vinegar
- ½ cup olive oil—the good stuff!

Directions:

- Boil potatoes whole in salted water until they are still firm but can be easily pierced through to the center with a knife. Drain potatoes.
- Sprinkle minced garlic with coarse salt and mash into paste on your cutting board using the flat edge of your knife. Whisk together with vinegar. Season with pepper.
- Mix mint and garlic scapes in a large bowl.
- Cut warm potatoes in 1" pieces—halved or quartered—and toss with mint and garlic scapes. The heat from the potatoes will release oils in the mint.
- Finish the vinaigrette: While whisking, drizzle oil into vinegar mixture. This will form a creamy emulsion.
- Toss vinaigrette with potatoes. Dress lightly so not to overpower the other flavors.
- Season to taste with salt, pepper and additional mint.

TIP: The sharp edges of coarse salt crystals are important. They make the task of shredding minced garlic down into a paste easy. Just drag the salt and garlic together across your cutting board with the flat edge of your knife.

FARMERS THINK WE'RE HILARIOUS

Garlic plants send up strap-like leaves each spring and begin to photosynthesize, capturing the energy of the sun and sending it down into its bulb. They also send up scapes, or flowering stems, just like daylilies.

If the buds at the end of those flowering stems were allowed to blossom, they would divert significant and valuable energy from fattening the bulb, which we hope to eat a few weeks later. Farmers know to cut these scapes off shortly after they appear, often discarding them as waste.

Prized for years by the cognoscenti, it is only recently that the sweet and sharp garlicy flavor of scapes became widely popular. They are delicious in pesto or blanched and stir-fried, and I use them each spring until fresh garlic is finally available.

I imagine farmers sitting on the porch at the end of each market day, drinking a cold one and smiling at their sales. Then I think about how little we pay for most of our food, and I smile, happy we give them this little win.

121

TIP: It's okay if your pork is a bit pink. The important thing for food safety is that the internal temperature reaches 145 while resting.

TIP: Broiling the meat 8" away from the heating element means the sugars have time to cook into a sticky, sweet glaze without burning.

HONEY & CHIVE GLAZED PORK

Serves 6-8

The earthy flavors of sweet honey and oniony chives give this pork a light, fresh flavor, perfect for a spring dinner or brunch. Make extra, it tastes great cold the next day for lunch.

Ingredients:

2 cups rice wine vinegar, divided
½ cup honey, divided
¼ cup plus 2 tbs olive oil
2 tbs Tamari soy sauce
1 cup minced chives, divided
4 cloves garlic, minced
1 tsp salt
½ tsp pepper
½ tsp cinnamon
1 package of two pork tenderloins
¼ cup brown sugar
1" ginger, peeled and cut in rounds

Directions:

- Whisk together 1 cup rice wine vinegar, ¼ cup honey, ¼ cup olive oil, soy sauce, ½ cup chives, garlic, salt, pepper and cinnamon.
- Place pork tenderloins in a freezer bag and add marinade. Marinate 2 hours to overnight.
- Remove tenderloins from bag, reserving marinade, and pat dry. Heat oven to 400 degrees.
- Heat 2 tbs oil in a 12" oven-proof skillet over medium-high heat. Add tenderloins and sear on all sides, tucking under the thin tails so the meat cooks evenly. Place skillet in oven and cook tenderloin to 135 degrees, about 15 minutes.
- While pork cooks, in a small sauce pan stir together remaining rice wine vinegar, honey and chives with brown sugar and ginger. Cook over medium-high heat until reduced to a syrupy glaze.
- Brush tenderloins with glaze, return to oven and broil on a rack set 8" from heat. Cook 2-3 minutes. Glaze again and cook 2-3 minutes longer, being careful not to burn the sugar. Remove pork from oven and reserve on a plate, tented with foil.
- Return skillet to medium-high and add marinade. Boil for 5 minutes, then whisk in any juices that have accumulated under the pork. Slice tenderloins and serve with sauce.

POKE IT!

Cooking meat to the right temperature is important for keeping you and your diners healthy and safe. The best way to do this is with an instant read thermometer. However, while sautéing, roasting and grilling, you may want to check the meat for doneness more frequently and quickly.

Next time you cook meat, whether it's pork tenderloin or a thick, juicy steak, poke it with your finger a few times while it cooks. Notice the texture it achieves when your thermometer tells you that it's reached a safe temperature. Over time, you'll get comfortable with how fully cooked, or undercooked, meat feels, saving that thermometer reading for right at the end. Go ahead, you really should play with your food.

123

SURPRISE!

One Easter morning when I was four or five, we hunted for jellybeans instead of eggs. File that away for later.

At fourteen, now a young boy with a flair for the dramatic, I decided to surprise my family with the biggest Easter egg hunt ever. Late Saturday night, I snuck out of the house after everyone had gone to bed. I rode my bike exactly one mile to the local Dairy Mart, where I purchased four dozen eggs, several coloring kits and one package of those plastic collars that shrink onto the egg when submerged in boiling water.

Back home, I hard-boiled and decorated each egg. They were dyed brightly, with "Mom", "Dad", "Katie" and "Alec" added using the clear, wax crayon. The Paas stickers, including a turtle and the little, golden cross, were carefully placed.

Well past midnight, I snuck quietly out into the backyard and hid each of those 48 eggs. I then crept up to my third floor bedroom and drifted off to sleep, smiling in anticipation of morning's big reveal.

I awoke Easter morning about an hour after my Dad. He was up early to let the dogs out. I rushed downstairs into the kitchen and announced, beaming, every detail of the prior night's mischief. Dad, looking worried, walked me out into the yard.

"Do you remember," he asked, "the year we had the jellybean hunt for Easter?"

"Of course," I replied. It was so cool. No one else I knew had ever hunted jellybeans.

"We had planned an outdoor Easter egg hunt that year, too," Dad said, "but when we let the dogs out, they ate each and every one of the eggs."

Sure enough, the eggs were gone. Every last one of them. All that remained were a few pieces of shell and those colorful plastic shrink-wraps, covered in chew marks.

Dad and I walked back inside, where he let me help hide the two-dozen eggs we had decorated as a family the afternoon before.

NOTE: For those of you worried about the dogs, our two labs were just fine, despite looking a bit smug.

TIP: Once the Panko breadcrumbs are toasted golden brown, remove them immediately from the pan. Like nuts and seeds, breadcrumbs will burn from the residual heat in your skillet.

GRILLED CHEESE & TOMATO SOUP OMELET

Makes 3 omelets

This is the ultimate breakfast comfort food. Sautéed tomatoes and sharp cheddar provide the soup and cheese for this omelet. Buttered panko breadcrumbs deliver the grilled cheese's toast.

For sauce:

- 2 tbs olive oil
- 1 large onion, diced
- 2 cloves garlic, minced
- 2 tomatoes, diced
- 1 tbs chopped parsley
- 2 tbs chopped basil
- 1 tbs chopped garlic chives
- 2 tbs olive oil—the good stuff!
- Sherry vinegar

For omelet

- 6 tbs butter, divided
- ½ cup Panko breadcrumbs
- 1 ⅓ cup grated sharp cheddar cheese
- 4 tsp cream, divided
- 8 eggs, divided

Directions:

- Warm oil in a 12" skillet over medium heat. Add onion and cook 5 minutes until softened. Add garlic and cook 2 minutes longer.

- Add tomatoes and cook until softened. Reduce and thicken, about 10 minutes, until still moist but not wet. Stir in fresh herbs and season to taste with salt, pepper and a splash of vinegar and olive oil. Remove from pan and reserve.

- Rinse pan and return to medium heat with 2 tbs butter. When butter has melted, add breadcrumbs and cook until lightly toasted. Remove from pan and reserve.

- Whisk together 2 eggs with 1 tsp cream and a pinch each of salt and pepper.

- Return pan to medium-low heat with 1 tbs butter. Melt butter, tilting pan to coat bottom and edges. Add eggs to pan and cook, undisturbed, until surface begins to set.

- Spread about ¼ of the tomato mixture on the third of the omelet closest to you. Sprinkle with ⅓ cup grated cheddar and about ¼ of the toasted breadcrumbs.

- Let cook 2 minutes longer, fold the omelet in thirds, and keep warm in the oven.

- Repeat with remaining ingredients to make 4 omelets.

THE PERFECT OMELET

While the French would tell you that a perfect omelet has no color on the bottom, my Dad prefers his crispy and brown. However you like yours, there are a few key points to getting an omelet just right. First, warm your pan for 2–3 minutes over heat set a little below medium.

Don't worry about a non-stick skillet. Coat the pan with melted butter and pour in your eggs. Once the edges set, you can run a heat-proof rubber spatula around the pan a couple of times but, other than that, leave them alone.

I always serve my omelets with the egg in the center still glistening and a little wet. Once the omelet is cooked through, the bottom will easily release—except for maybe a small spot in the middle. If it comes out looking like a total mess, just remember, it's your breakfast table and not a gallery in the Louvre. I bet it tastes delicious!

TIP: If you substitute a less fatty meat (like turkey bacon) for the pancetta,
make sure to add some olive oil or more butter before pouring in your
eggs or the frittata will stick to the pan.

128

WILD MUSHROOM & GRUYERE FRITTATA

Serves 6

Rich wild mushrooms and sharp Gruyere are beautifully balanced in this thick Italian omelet, puffed and golden from a quick finish under the broiler.

Ingredients:

2 tbs butter

2 shallots, minced

2 cloves garlic, minced

2 cups sliced wild mushrooms

1 tbs chopped thyme

2 tbs dry Sherry

¼ pound pancetta

6 eggs

3 tbs whole milk

1 cup shaved Gruyere cheese

½ cup shaved Parmesan cheese

Directions:

‣ Melt butter in a large skillet over medium heat.

‣ Add shallot and cook until soft, about 5 minutes. Add garlic and cook until fragrant, about 1 minute.

‣ Add mushrooms and thyme. Cook until mushrooms are golden on edges.

‣ Deglaze skillet with 2 tbs Sherry. Remove mushrooms and reserve.

‣ Return skillet to medium heat and sauté pancetta until crispy about 5 minutes. Sprinkle the mushrooms evenly over the pan.

‣ Lightly whisk together eggs, milk and Gruyere. Pour over pancetta and mushrooms and tilt pan to evenly distribute.

‣ Cook over medium heat until almost set. To finish, sprinkle with Parmesan and set under broiler until puffy and golden, 1–2 minutes.

TIP: Don't play with the egg! Once you pour them into the pan, leave your eggs alone. They will lightly brown on the bottom and easily release when they come out of the oven.

PUTTING IT TOGETHER: MUSHROOM MADNESS

After a long winter, spring heralds the playoff season for sports from college basketball to hockey. Whether you have a favorite team or just want to bring home bragging rights by winning the office pool, you'll need some hearty dishes to sustain you during night after night of nail-biting excitement. Earthy, rich mushrooms will keep you going. I even added some steak. And the potatoes? You know you're going to ask for some. I'm just beating you to the punch.

Sirloin, Asparagus & Portabellas with Béarnaise (page 105)

Fiddlehead Tacos (page 117)

Wild Mushroom & Gruyere Frittata

Potatoes with Peanut Sauce & Spinach (page 99)

EGG FU YUNG

Serves 6–8

This Chinese take-out classic is typically a bit watery and buried beneath a gelatinous brown gravy. Fresh ingredients and a homemade sauce transform it into a fresh-tasting, special treat. Add some lightly browned pork sausage if you prefer yours with meat.

For sauce:

- 2 tbs corn starch
- 3 tbs Tamari soy sauce
- 2 tbs apple cider vinegar
- 1 tbs Sherry vinegar
- 1 tbs sesame oil
- 1 ½ cups vegetable stock

For omelet:

- 6 eggs
- 1 tbs sesame oil
- 3 scallions, thinly sliced
- 4 tbs peanut or vegetable oil
- 2 cups cabbage, thinly sliced
- 1 ½ cups Shitake mushrooms, sliced thin
- 2 cloves garlic, minced

Directions:

- Mix together sauce ingredients in a small saucepan and simmer until thickened. Keep warm.

- Whisk together eggs, sesame oil and green parts of scallions in a large bowl.

- On medium-high heat, warm 1 tbs peanut oil in a 12" skillet. Add white part of scallions and cook until softened, about 1 minute. Add cabbage and stir-fry until tender but still firm. Remove from skillet and stir into the egg mixture.

- Return skillet to medium heat, add 1 tbs peanut oil and Shitake mushrooms. Sauté until softened and browning on edges. Add garlic and cook for 30 seconds more. Remove from skillet and stir into egg mixture.

- Heat 2 tbs peanut oil in skillet over medium-low heat. Pour in eggs, cover and cook. When top is set, serve with sauce.

TIP: Egg fu yung is typically made with mung bean sprouts for a little crunch. Usually overcooked, they just end up being watery. Don't make the same mistake with your cabbage. Leave it crisp-tender.

INSIDE, UNDER, MIXED TOGETHER

What's the difference between omelets, frittatas and egg fu yung? With omelets, you begin cooking the egg first and fold the other ingredients (cheese, vegetables and meat) inside. With a frittata, you cook the additional ingredients and pour the egg over them. For egg fu yung, the eggs and filling are stirred together before being returned to the skillet and cooked through. A Spanish tortilla, is made the same way, combining lightly-whisked eggs with fried potatoes and cooking them together in a skillet.

However they are assembled, these egg dishes are perfect one-pan meals for breakfast, lunch or dinner—and a great way to use leftover meats and vegetables.

PERFECT POSSIBILITY

In my mind, each and every sunny day beginning in June is exactly like this one, perfect Saturday morning at my family's farmhouse in Western Massachusetts. It's 7:30, maybe 8:00 and I'm standing barefoot in dew soaked grass holding a cup of black coffee.

The air is thick and slow without any of the humidity that will creep in throughout the morning. The sun is warm, birds sing lazily and insects buzz as I walk out past the barn, ducking under the clothes line, and pass around the vegetable garden to the strawberries. I fill a bowl to the brim, while eating almost as many as I harvest.

In this perfect moment the possibilities are endless. This day stretches ahead of me filled with seemingly unconflicting opportunities to weed gardens, harvest green beans and deadhead roses. I can hike in the woods, swim in ponds, and bike for miles. The kitchen beckons with pancakes for breakfast, fresh garden lettuce and slightly sun warmed cucumbers for lunch. I could marinate meat for grilling, juice plums for a granita, and fry thick rounds of fresh zucchini dipped in egg and breadcrumbs when it comes time for dinner.

Back at the house I open the screen door, step inside, greet my parents and turn on Ibrahim Ferrer who will sing us through breakfast. The day's endless opportunities begin to fade and contract as plans are made, schedules set. The perfect possibility of the day ahead remains only until the last pancake has been eaten and the sound of the first mower breaks the morning's peace.

JONATHAN BARDZIK

133

TIP: Let the batter rest for 10 minutes after combining the wet and dry ingredients. This gives the baking soda time to activate and begin foaming, creating light, fluffy pancakes.

STRAWBERRY PANCAKES
WITH RHUBARB SYRUP

Serves 4–6

While I have no argument with eating pie for breakfast, here's another sweet way to put strawberries and rhubarb on a lazy Sunday morning table.

For syrup:

- 2 cups chopped rhubarb stalks, cut into ½" pieces
- 1 ½ cups real maple syrup

For pancakes:

- 1 vanilla bean
- ½ cup whole milk
- 1 ½ cups buttermilk
- 2-3 sprigs lemon balm
- 2 cups flour
- 4 tsp sugar
- 1 tsp salt
- 1 tsp baking powder
- ½ tsp baking soda
- ½ tsp cardamom
- 2 eggs, separated
- 4 tbs butter, melted and slightly cooled
- 1 pint strawberries, sliced thinly

Directions:

- In small saucepan, combine rhubarb and maple syrup. Simmer over low heat for 20 minutes. Keep warm.

- Slice open vanilla bean and scrape seeds into small saucepan with milk, buttermilk and lemon balm. Add bean and bring to a simmer over medium heat. Remove from heat and let steep 20 minutes. Strain infused milk into a bowl, discarding solids.

- In a small bowl, whisk together egg yolks and butter. Pour into infused milk and whisk to combine. Whisk in egg whites.

- In a large bowl, whisk together flour, sugar, salt, baking powder and cardamom. Stir liquid ingredients into dry ingredients. Let stand for 10 minutes.

- Set your stove burner just below medium heat and warm 1 tbs vegetable oil in a large skillet. Pour batter into pan for pancakes, about ⅓ cup each.

- Top each pancake with strawberry slices, turning when pancake bottoms are lightly browned. Cook 1 minute longer.

- Serve pancakes topped with rhubarb syrup.

WHEN TO FLIP YOUR PANCAKES

Flipping pancakes can seem like a difficult art to master, often resulting in splattering batter or pancakes that fall apart. The key is to let the pancake batter cook through sufficiently before trying to turn them.

Start by warming your pan for 3–4 minutes over a burner set just below medium. When you add your batter, watch for bubbles to appear on the surface. At first, they will break through and the batter will close back over them. When several of the holes remain open, flip your pancake and cook it for just 1 minute longer before removing it from the pan. If the pancakes are too brown on the bottom when you flip them, turn down your heat slightly and wait a minute before starting the next batch.

TIP: Stir in the cheese right before serving or it will settle to
the bottom of the pan and stick there.

PASTA PRIMAVERA

Serves 6

This is Primavera with truly seasonal, bright spring ingredients. A sauce of sweet cream is light yet rich without dulling the farm-fresh vegetables.

Ingredients:

1 ½ cups chopped asparagus, in 2" pieces

1 ½ cups halved snow peas

3 tbs olive oil, divided

5 cloves garlic, minced, divided

⅛ tsp red pepper flakes, divided

2 cups halved cherry tomatoes

Aged balsamic vinegar

½ pound farfalle or fettuccini

2 tbs butter

5–6 large Shitake mushrooms, sliced

¾ cup cream

½ cup grated Parmesan cheese

¼ cup toasted pine nuts

Directions:

- Cook asparagus and snow peas: In 6 quart pot of salted boiling water, blanch asparagus for 2 minutes. Add snow peas. Cook 1 minute longer. Remove to ice bath leaving cooking water in the pot.

- Warm 2 tbs oil in a 12" skillet over medium-low heat. Sauté half the garlic and half of the pepper flakes until garlic turns golden. Add blanched asparagus and snow peas to skillet. Sauté 2 minutes longer. Remove vegetables from pan and reserve.

- Cook tomatoes: Return pan to medium heat with remaining 1 tbs oil. Add remaining pepper flakes and garlic. Cook 30 seconds, until fragrant. Add tomatoes, increase heat to medium, and cook until softened, 5-7 minutes. Deglaze pan with 1-2 tbs aged balsamic vinegar. Reserve.

- Cook mushrooms and begin sauce: Return skillet to medium heat and add butter to melt. Add mushrooms and cook until softened. Add cream and bring to a simmer.

- Cook pasta: Boil pasta in vegetable water until slightly firmer than al dente, lightly undercooked. Drain, reserving 1 cup cooking liquid.

- Finish the sauce: Add pasta and cooking water to the cream in the skillet. Simmer until thickened. Stir in cheese.

- Combine components: Toss pasta with asparagus and snow peas. Serve topped with tomatoes, additional cheese and pine nuts.

COMPOUND RECIPES

Recipes like Pasta Primavera can make our head explode. It seems like there are too many steps and components to keep track of—a culinary version of Who's on First. The challenge is in visualizing the components. First, there are the fresh green vegetables—asparagus and snow peas—to blanch and sauté. Next, we make a quick balsamic tomato sauce. Our third step is to make the mushroom cream sauce, which we use (along with added pasta cooking liquid) to finish cooking the pasta. The dish is finished by adding cheese and returning the green vegetables to the pan. It is served topped with the sautéed tomatoes, toasted pine nuts, and more cheese, because...well, because. Visualize those components a few times before starting the recipe, and it will be a breeze—a fresh, spring one.

TIP: The tough, crumbly, nearly inedible scones from the coffee counter are a
    tragically poor representation of this delicate, light biscuit. Work quickly,
    handling the dough as little as possible, for delightfully tender scones. And
    make sure that butter is cold!

STRAWBERRY SHORTCAKE WITH CARDAMOM SCONES

Serves 6–8

Elevate this classic spring dessert with tender, handmade scones and minted whipped cream. No one needs to know it took you less than 15 minutes from scratch to get the scones in the oven. Special thanks to Genevieve O'Sullivan, co-owner of Sona Creamery, for her amazing scone recipe!

For berries:

- 2 pints strawberries, hulled and halved
- 3 tbs sugar
- ¼ cup Grand Mariner

For cream:

- 1 cup cream
- 2 tbs chopped mint

For scones:

- 3 cups flour
- ¼ cup sugar
- 2 ½ tsp baking powder
- ½ tsp baking soda
- ¾ tsp salt
- ¼ tsp cardamom
- ¾ cup butter cut in 2" pieces
- 1 cup buttermilk

BY HAND

Electric kitchen appliances may save time and work, but there is no better way to learn your ingredients than working by hand. You may go back to using the electric beaters, but whisking cream, egg whites and even custard is the best way to learn that moment when the texture, volume and moisture are perfect. Whipped cream hits the peak of perfection—light and airy, yet still moist—less than twenty strokes before it becomes dry and grainy. That's a hard target to hit with beaters, but an easy one with a whisk. Whisking by hand is when you most value sharing time in the kitchen with good friends; because that's when you put them to work.

Directions:

- Preheat oven to 400 degrees.
- Mix together strawberries, 2 tbs sugar and liqueur. Place in refrigerator to macerate, releasing their natural juices.
- Make scones: Add flour, sugar, baking powder, baking soda, salt and cardamom in a large bowl. Whisk to combine.
- Toss butter on top of flour mixture. Cut butter in using a pastry cutter or two knives until the mixture resembles breadcrumbs.
- Make well in center of dough and add buttermilk. Stir 15 times until the liquid is just incorporated.
- Remove dough from bowl and place on lightly floured countertop. Knead dough 5–7 turns until it just comes together.
- Shape into two 6" rounds and cut into quarters. Place on an ungreased baking sheet and bake for 16 minutes. When golden brown on top, remove from oven and cool on a wire rack.
- Make minted cream: Sprinkle mint with remaining 1 tbs sugar and chop until very fine. Place cream in a medium bowl and whisk until soft peaks form. Sprinkle minted sugar over the top and whisk 15–20 strokes more for stiff, airy, moist peaks.
- Slice scones in half, place bottom in a bowl, stir together strawberries to coat with juice and spoon liberally over. Top with scone top halves and a giant, delicious dollop of whipped cream.

SWEET ENOUGH

My Babci (my Polish grandmother) grew rhubarb plants on the edge of her large garden, near a maple tree where we would sit and eat lunch during the summer at a red-stained picnic table. My Mom's rhubarb plants sit on the back edge of the garden near the blueberry bushes. They are planted there because rhubarb returns each year, from its roots, and you don't want to accidentally till it up when turning your soil in the spring.

At home, in Western Massachusetts, the bright red stalks ripen in early June, about the same time we go strawberry picking. Mom baked pies with hers. My great aunt Mary, made quick jam with rhubarb and strawberry Jello. Babci gave us cups of sugar into which we'd dip the stalks and eat them raw.

Rhubarb is sharply bitter. Even with sugar it elicits a pucker. Cooked down into a thick, jammy chutney, I could still not imagine it without the balance of brown sugar.

But somehow in this relish with no sugar at all, it works. Balanced by ripe, sweet cherries and grounded with earthy shallot, bright with vinegar and warmed by cardamom, it sits perfectly alongside rich meats—pork chops, grilled steaks or sausages.

You can use your food processor, but I chop it by hand. I like the texture and it keeps the flavors clearer. Besides, the extra few minutes in the kitchen provide a little time to chat, listen to music, or just enjoy the warm, late spring breeze coming in the window.

RHUBARB CHERRY RELISH

Makes 1 ¾ cups

Sweet cherries offer surprising balance to tart rhubarb while a splash of white balsamic vinegar keeps it clean and bright. Try it served with grilled steak or sausages.

Ingredients:

½ cup finely chopped rhubarb stalks
1 cup finely chopped cherries
¼ cup minced shallot
2 tsp minced basil
1 ½ tsp white balsamic vinegar
2 tsp ruby red grapefruit juice
Cardamom

Directions:

- Combine rhubarb, cherries and shallot in a medium bowl.
- Stir in basil and vinegar and grapefruit juice.
- Season to taste with a pinch each of cardamom and salt.

PUTTING IT TOGETHER: NEARLY SUMMER

The days are getting long, you're wearing shorts, and can even work up a little sweat while sipping wine on the patio after work. Summer is nearly here and while its bright, bold produce hasn't yet arrived, you can still gather friends around the grill, crack open a few beers and enjoy a meal together.

Grilled steaks with Rhubarb Cherry Relish
Baby arugula with an Early Tomato Vinaigrette (page 147)
Minted Garlic Scape Potato Salad (page 121)
Strawberry Shortcake with Cardamom Scones (page 139)

TIP: If you make this ahead of time, check seasoning right before serving. As juices develop you may find you want a pinch more of salt or cardamom or a little more fresh basil.

STRAWBERRY AVOCADO SALSA
WITH SALMON

Serves 4 with leftover salsa

*Creamy, rich avocado and sweet strawberries are brightened with a splash
of lime juice and just the right kick from a little jalapeño. You'll be putting
this on pork and fish, scooping it up with chips, or just spooning it directly
into your mouth.*

Ingredients:

2 cups strawberries, hulled and chopped

1 large avocado, diced

1 shallot, minced

½ tsp lime zest

¼ cup chopped cilantro

½ tsp finely minced jalapeño

Juice of ½ lime

1 tsp sugar

White balsamic vinegar

4 7-8 ounce salmon filets, skin on

4 tbs butter, cut in 4 pieces

Directions:

- Mix together strawberries, avocado, shallot, lime zest, cilantro
  and jalapeño.

- Dress with lime juice and sugar.

- Season to taste with a splash of vinegar and a pinch of salt.
  Refrigerate.

- Pat salmon filets dry and season with salt and pepper.

- Heat a 12" skillet over medium-high heat. Add butter to pan
  and melt.

- Add salmon, filets skin-side down. Press down on each filet with
  a spatula for 20–30 seconds to sear skin evenly.

- After 5–6 minutes the flesh will turn pink and firm. Serve
  topped with salsa.

FROM A DISTANCE

*There's no question that I love locally-
grown, farm-fresh seasonal food for
it's amazing flavor, but there are some
ingredients I love to eat that will never be
farmed in the Mid-Atlantic or Western
Massachusetts.*

*So, when do I enjoy pineapples,
artichokes and avocado? When they are
in season. Even shipped across country
from California or across the Pacific from
Hawaii, these ingredients taste best when
they are seasonal and fresh, at the peak
of their growing season. So enjoy your
pineapples and artichokes in March through
May. California's avocados are fortunately
in season from March through early
September, so you can scoop your chips in
their creamy, rich goodness all summer long.*

TIP: Lime juice not only brightens the sweet strawberries and
    rich buttery avocados but keeps them from turning brown.

EARLY TOMATO VINAIGRETTE

Makes 1 ¼ cups

Grated tomato infuses this vinaigrette with bright flavor without any thick chunks. Perfect for the first hothouse tomatoes fresh from the farm.

Ingredients:

1 medium tomato
1 clove garlic
3–4 large basil leaves, cut into thin ribbons
¼ cup red wine vinegar
¾ cup olive oil—the good stuff

Directions:

- Cut tomato in half, scoop out seeds with your fingers. Grate on a box grater, cut side against the grate. The tough skin of the tomato will protect your hand from the sharp edge of the grater.

- Sprinkle minced garlic with coarse salt and mash into paste on your cutting board using the flat edge of your knife.

- Whisk together garlic paste, ⅓ cup tomato pulp, basil and vinegar. Season with black pepper.

- While whisking, drizzle oil into vinegar mixture to form a creamy emulsion.

- Season to taste with salt, pepper and more vinegar or oil.

UNDER COVER TOMATO

The first fresh tomatoes that appear at the farm market have probably been grown under cover, giving them a jump start on the season. However, before you group them in with the grocery store hot-house tomato— their flavorless, rock hard relatives—take another taste.

While they will never have the bright, bold sugars and acidity of a tomato at the peak of summer, they do have the benefit of having been grown in rich soil and fully ripened on the vine. On top of that, it's been eight months since you've had a good garden-fresh tomato. These are going to taste amazing!

TIP: If the tomatoes aren't sweet enough yet, add a drizzle of honey.

STRAWBERRY & SHAVED FENNEL SALAD

Serves 6

This light, crisp, sweet salad is the perfect side for your Memorial Day cookout. Serve it on its own, or over fresh greens like baby spinach or butter lettuce.

For dressing:

- 1 shallot, minced
- 1 tsp sugar
- ½ tsp Dijon mustard
- ⅓ cup white balsamic vinegar
- ⅔ cup grape seed or vegetable oil

For salad:

- 2 cups hulled and sliced strawberries
- 2 fennel bulbs, cored and thinly sliced
- 1 tbs fennel fronds, finely chopped
- 2 tbs finely chopped mint leaves
- ¼ cup toasted pepitas (hulled pumpkin seeds)

Directions:

- In a medium bowl, combine shallot, sugar, mustard and vinegar with a pinch of salt. Whisk together.
- Combine strawberries, fennel, fennel fronds and mint in a separate bowl. Toss together.
- While whisking, add oil to vinegar in a thin stream, to form a creamy emulsion.
- Taste dressing with a forkful of fennel and strawberry. Season dressing to taste with additional sugar or vinegar and toss with salad. Sprinkle with toasted pepitas and serve.

TIP: Fennel has a hard, white, cone-shaped core. To remove it, quarter the fennel and cut out the core before thinly slicing the more tender bulb.

TIP: Pepitas are hulled and roasted pumpkin seeds. Look for them in with other seeds, nuts and dried fruits in your grocery store. If you cannot find them, try substituting toasted sunflower seeds or pine nuts.

RED, WHITE AND WALDORF

This is my take on the classic American salad created at its namesake New York City hotel near the end of the 19th century. Crisp, fresh fennel stands in for celery while sweet, spring strawberries replace fall apples. Toasted pumpkin seeds replace earthy walnuts and a white balsamic vinaigrette offers a lighter alternative to the traditional mayonnaise dressing. So maybe, after all, this has nothing at all to do with a Waldorf salad—but it did provide exquisite inspiration.

summer

THE GOOD LIFE.

The first job I took after college was with Quansett Nurseries, selling plants to garden centers. Owner Fred Dabney's property reaches right out to Buzzard's Bay, a quiet stretch of salt water between Rhode Island and Cape Cod. Through the woods adjoining Fred's property, is Sylvan Nurseries, owned at the time by his good friend and customer Neil Van Sloun.

A couple of times each spring, during our busy selling and shipping season between Memorial Day and Father's Day, Fred would leave my fellow salesman Scott and me alone in the office to spend the day with Neil on his fishing boat. Sitting out on the water, Fred and Neil would pull up lobster traps, talk shop, and, I have to imagine, tip back a couple of cold beers.

Although Scott and I wanted desperately to be annoyed by this, the two nurserymen did a lot of business out on that boat. While hauling traps they would monitor walkie-talkie chatter from back at their respective offices.

"I've got a customer looking for a hundred and fifty pots of creeping phlox," a salesman at Sylvan might say.

Fred, listening in, would call back to the office, telling us to add those hundred and fifty phlox to a trailer. By the end of the day, the trailer would be completely

filled with Sylvan's orders, which we would drive through the woods and deliver.

After one particularly successful day of selling, Fred returned to the office shortly after closing time. There he found two rather irked salesmen ready to head home for the night. A broad grin broke across Fred's face, from underneath his mustache. He raised up his hand holding a mesh bag filled with oysters that he and Neil had pulled up along with the lobster traps.

Scott immediately pulled a bottle of Jack Daniels from above one of the drop ceiling tiles (whose existence I was, until that moment, completely unaware of). Fred removed a bottle of hot sauce from the bottom drawer of his desk, and with his slightly rusty pocket knife—the kind every nurserywoman and man carries at all times—began shucking oysters. We sat there, afternoon sunshine streaming in the screen door of the dusty office, laughing easily, and slurping down one of the ocean's great delicacies, wiping wet hands on our jeans.

These were my first oysters. None that have followed, served on silver trays of ice with mignonette—a sauce I couldn't even pronounce at the time—and horse-radish, have tasted as salty and sweet.

That, for me, is the true joy of summer. Taking in the very best that life can offer—bold, bright produce, fresh from the farm and garden, served alongside rich meats and briny fish, slightly charred from the grill; enjoyed outside together with good friends and family, while your bare toes wiggle in the grass.

So slip into your Sunday morning shorts and pull on your best T-shirt. Summer's here and it's time to live the good life. There'll be plenty of time for hard work later.

JONATHAN BARDZIK

CUCUMBER DILL MOUSSE

Serves 6–8

Dill infused whipped cream lightens grated cucumber, fresh mint and earthy chives into an airy summer delight. Serve it in a bread bowl with crisp vegetables, as a sauce over grilled salmon, or to garnish hand-cut gazpacho.

Ingredients:

- 2 small cucumbers
- 1 tsp salt, divided
- ½ shallot, minced
- 1 tsp finely chopped mint
- 1 tbs finely chopped chives
- 1 tbs red wine vinegar
- ¼ tsp hot Hungarian paprika
- 2 tbs chopped dill
- 1 cup heavy or whipping cream

Directions:

- Peel and seed cucumbers. Grate on the small side of a box grater. Place in a mesh sieve set over a bowl and sprinkle with ½ tsp salt to draw out water. Let stand for 20 minutes, then press to remove liquid.

- In a medium bowl, mix together shallot, mint, chives, vinegar and paprika. Season to taste with black pepper.

- Add cucumber to shallot and herb mixture. Stir together well and season to taste with salt and additional vinegar.

- On a cutting board, sprinkle chopped dill with ½ tsp salt and finely chop together.

- Whisk cream to soft peaks in a medium bowl. Add salted dill and whisk cream to stiff peaks, another 20–25 strokes.

- Stir ¼ of the whipped cream into cucumber mixture to lighten. Fold in remaining cream.

TIP: To seed the cucumbers, cut them in half after peeling, and scoop out the seeds with a teaspoon.

TIP: To whip cream, you need a minimum of 30% fat content. Heavy or whipping cream will both work. Avoid ultra-pasteurized cream. The process damages whey proteins making it harder to whip to stiff peaks.

SWEET AND SAVORY INSPIRATION

Three years ago, cooking a mid-summer dinner for friends, I was hit by inspiration to combine blueberries and peaches with cardamom, Thai basil and whipped cream. I tossed the sweet, ripe fruit with the ground spice. Taking my lead from garlic paste, made by mashing together coarse salt and minced garlic, I finely chopped together sharp-edged, crystalline sugar and Thai basil then whisked it into whipped cream.

Last year, reflecting on that dish, I wondered—could I make a savory whipped cream with fresh herbs? I wondered whether salt or vinegar would weaken the delicate suspension of air in cream, but my fears were unfounded and a summer-weight version of leaden sour-cream dips was born. In my kitchen, at room temperature, the mousse has held overnight, still light and airy (if not particularly appealing) the next morning. I'd suggest putting leftovers in the fridge.

TIP: Farm and garden-fresh, ripe tomatoes will release plenty of liquid to steam
the squash and reduce to a coating sauce. If your tomatoes seem dryer, add
a half cup of water to the pan when you add the squash.

SUMMER SQUASH GOULASH

Serves 6

Earthy mushrooms, rich tomato paste and bold miso paste turn light, garden-fresh vegetables into a hearty, one-dish summer meal. No one at your table will miss the meat.

Ingredients:

2 tbs olive oil
1 large onion, diced
2 cloves garlic, minced
2 cups thinly sliced Crimini mushrooms
1 red pepper, diced
2 tbs sweet paprika
2 tbs tomato paste
2 tbs red miso paste
2 tomatoes, seeded and diced
2 cups halved and thinly sliced summer squash
¼ cup chopped basil
Sherry vinegar

Directions:

- In a sauté pan over medium heat, cook onion in olive oil until softened. Add garlic and cook 30 seconds until fragrant.
- Add mushrooms and cook until lightly browned on edges.
- Add red pepper, paprika, tomato paste and miso paste. Cook 1–2 minutes until paprika is fragrant.
- Stir in tomatoes and cook until they begin to soften and release their liquid.
- Add squash and basil. Cover and cook until squash is softened but still firm.
- Uncover and let thicken to desired consistency.
- Season to taste with salt, pepper and vinegar.

GOING VEGETARIAN

Five or six years ago, my husband Jason and I went vegetarian. It was a great three months.

No, we didn't last long but that wasn't really the point. Bored with cooking the same things, I turned to a vegetarian diet to learn new recipes and ingredients. It worked! First, thanks to cookbook authors like Molly Katzen and Deborah Madison, I was introduced to ways of layering in the rich, umami flavors we associate with meat using ingredients like mushrooms, miso and tomato pastes.

Secondly, I changed how I think about constructing a meal. Originally, I tried to replace the meat based main dish with a vegetable, egg or dairy based option. But, taking a cue from international vegetarian cultures, I learned to explore a range from one-dish meals to several evenly weighted dishes with bright, bold condiments.

Today, we eat less meat, but more importantly, our meals are far more interesting and varied. And yes, I still eat bacon.

PEACH BLUEBERRY SALSA

Makes about 6 cups

Though sweetened by peaches and blueberries, the acidity in the fruit, tomatoes and vinegar keep this salsa savory enough to serve over a grilled chicken breast or pork chop, or simply with a big bowl of chips.

Ingredients:

- 4 peaches, peeled and diced
- 1 ½ cups blueberries
- 1 tomato, diced
- 1 medium cucumber, peeled, seeded and diced
- 1 small red onion, diced
- 1 tbs olive oil—the good stuff!
- 1 tbs white balsamic vinegar
- 1 tbs honey
- 1 tbs minced tarragon
- 1 tbs chopped basil
- ¼ tsp cayenne pepper
- ¼ tsp cardamom
- White pepper

Directions:

- Mix together peaches, blueberries, tomato, cucumber and red onion.
- Add olive oil, vinegar, honey, tarragon, basil, cayenne pepper and cardamom. Toss through to blend.
- Before serving, season to taste with a pinch of salt, white pepper and additional honey.

TIP: The honey brings out the fruit flavors. If your berries and peaches are more acidic, you'll need more honey to balance them.

(UNA)PEELING PEACHES

The blanching method for peeling peaches never fails to thoroughly frustrate me, sending half-peeled, mushy peaches to the compost pile while I eat fresh berries instead.

If you absolutely, positively have to peel your peaches, here's the answer:

When I first moved to DC, my parents came to visit. We walked Eastern Market for hours. Mom looked at lots of jewelry that, being a thrifty New Englander, she decided she didn't really need. Then, we came upon Bob demonstrating his amazing peeler. It could tackle a Butternut squash and was delicate enough to peel a peach. Mom pulled out $9 and decided to bring one home.

No sooner had they returned home than I received a call. "This is amazing! Go back to the Market and buy three more for my sisters for Christmas." I figured Mom was onto something and bought one for me, too. I'm still using it today.

If you're at the Market this weekend, you'll find Bob's wife Tracy, demonstrating the peelers. You should say "hi"—and bring one home too.

159

TIP: If you can't find cardamom pods, just add a half-teaspoon of
ground cardamom. You could add a half-teaspoon of ground
cloves instead of the whole.

BOURBON PEACH PORK SHOULDER

Serves 8

Falling off the bone tender, this braised, rich cut of pork fills your mouth with sweet peaches and molasses, tart, acidic nectarines and vinegar, earthy soy and bright, complex spices.

Ingredients:

    2 tbs vegetable oil
    One bone-in pork shoulder roast, 4 to 5 pounds
    1 large onion, halved and thinly sliced
    2 cloves garlic, minced
    2 large peaches, sliced
    2 nectarines, sliced
    ½ cup cider vinegar
    ½ cup good bourbon
    ¼ cup Tamari soy sauce
    ¼ cup molasses, preferably light, unsulphured
    4 whole cloves
    3 cardamom pods
    1 tbs dry mustard
    2 tbs brown sugar

Directions:

- Warm 2 tbs olive oil in a Dutch oven over medium-high heat. Pat roast dry. Season with salt and pepper. Add to pot and brown well on all sides, about 15 minutes total. Remove from pot and reserve.

- Drain all but 2 tbs fat from the pot and return to medium heat. Add onions with a pinch of salt and cook until they beginning to caramelize, about 10 minutes. Add garlic and fruit and cook 5 minutes longer.

- Add vinegar, bourbon, soy sauce, molasses, cloves, cardamom pods and mustard to pot. Bring to a boil, scraping any brown bits from the bottom of the pot.

- Return pork to pot. Cover and place in a 250 degree oven for 6–8 hours.

- Remove from oven and place pork on a rimmed plate. Skim fat from sauce, then simmer for five minutes until reduced. Add in any additional juices from the platter of pork.

- Season to taste with sugar, salt and an additional splash of vinegar. Serve pork with sauce.

PICKING A BONE

There are two things you should know about the phrase "falling off the bone." First, to fall off the bone, you've got to buy a pork shoulder with the bone still inside. Why? While bones may add little flavor to quickly cooked meats (although they may have other benefits from texture to the simple joy of chewing on the bones at the end of your meal), their marrow adds wonderful flavor to slow braises.

Secondly—and somehow this always catches me off guard—the meat does actually fall off the bone. Unlike a roast, after hours of slow braising in the oven the long, low heat breaks down the connective tissues in this cut of pork, which means it won't hold together prettily for presentation on a platter. But no one will care, because it just tastes so good.

MOM WAS VERY, VERY RIGHT

When Mom said we were having a vegetable for dinner—say zucchini or green beans—it was, typically, just that. They were steamed, seasoned with salt and pepper, and possibly tossed with fresh herbs, usually parsley or basil from the garden. If Mom felt the rest of the meal was sufficiently healthy, she would add a small pat of butter. This, it turns out, is a fabulous way to serve almost any vegetable.

I should have been less surprised, I suppose, by the overwhelming success of a recent attempt at zucchini pasta. I think it was the "pasta" that misled me. I mean, I have trouble thinking that sautéed strips of squash are in any way going to deliver the deep satisfaction of semolina spaghetti. I was wrong. (And, because I would never hear the end of it from my husband, let's keep that little admission just between us.*)

The long strips that I quickly shaved with a vegetable peeler resembled wide pappardelle noodles. Cooked over low heat to keep the flavor light, I tossed in garlic and a splash of lemon juice, fresh basil and a grating of Parmesan cheese.

It was really good. But, I thought, I should try another batch, this one with chopped, fresh tomato. Then I made a third panful to confirm that it was just as good without the tomato. The fourth pan I cooked was to photograph. I am currently planning a fifth batch to serve under chicken piccata and a sixth for shrimp scampi. This is just for testing of course. I'm doing it all for you.

Summer's abundance gives us endless opportunity to experiment and invent. With a seemingly endless bounty the possibilities are limitless. Sometimes, however, simple is simply best.

*You know, just to be on the safe side, I'm going to retract any admission that I was wrong. Let's simply say that my Mom was very, very right.

ZUCCHINI PAPPARDELLE PASTA

Serves 4–6 as a side dish

Wide ribbons of thinly sliced zucchini, simply flavored with bright summer garlic, fresh herbs and a splash of lemon are delicious on their own or topped with grilled chicken and a quick tomato sauce.

Ingredients:

   2 tbs olive oil—the good stuff!

   2 small zucchini, sliced lengthwise into thin ribbons (See tip)

   2 cloves garlic, minced

   1 tbs chopped parsley

   1 tbs chopped basil

   1–2 tbs lemon juice

   ⅓ cup grated Parmesan cheese

Directions:

- Warm 1 tbs oil over medium heat in a 12" skillet. Add zucchini and sauté, turning often with tongs, for about 2 minutes.

- Add garlic and cook until zucchini is softened, 2–3 minutes longer.

- Mix in parsley, basil, lemon juice and remaining 1 tbs olive oil, tossing to coat zucchini.

- Season to taste with salt and pepper and serve topped with Parmesan cheese.

PUTTING IT TOGETHER: BOAT SHOES, HOLD THE SOCKS

There's something wonderful about dressing up in the summer. No matter how fine the occasion, the rules relax around the edges. Light cotton sundresses keep women cool while men's blazers are donned as a nod, discarded soon after arrival. But at summer gatherings, we celebrate with our feet as much as with bright, fresh, simple food. Sandals or boat shoes please, and hold the socks.

Grilled Chicken with
Cilantro Red Onion Salsa
(page 217)
Zucchini Pappardelle Pasta
Fresh Herbed Tomato Salad (page 169)

TIP: This would be the perfect time to break out your mandolin, but I make my ribbons quickly and easily with a good vegetable peeler. You won't be able to slice the entire zucchini. Just toss the leftovers in a bag and sauté or steam them for dinner tomorrow.

RANCH DRESSING

Makes 1 ½ cups

There's a reason this creamy, tangy, fresh herbal dressing gained national prominence. One batch of homemade will remind you just how good Ranch can and should be.

Ingredients:

1 egg
1 tsp Dijon mustard
2 tbs lemon juice
1 cup vegetable or grape seed oil
¼ cup crème fraîche
1 cup well-shaken buttermilk
1 clove garlic, chopped
2 tbs chopped parsley
2 tbs chopped chives
¼ cup additional chopped fresh herbs including
     tarragon, dill and cilantro
1 tsp chili powder
Cayenne pepper
Champagne vinegar

Directions:

- Place egg, mustard and lemon juice in a food processor. Season with a pinch of salt and pulse 5–6 times for 2–3 seconds each.

- Next, while processor is running, drizzle oil in a thin stream until thick mayonnaise forms. Season to taste with additional salt and lemon juice.

- Leave ¼ cup mayonnaise in the food processor. Remove the rest and save for another use.

- Add crème fraîche, buttermilk, garlic, fresh herbs, chili powder and a pinch of cayenne to the processor. Process until smooth and creamy.

- Season to taste with additional salt, black pepper, cayenne and a splash of vinegar.

TIP: The cayenne and vinegar provide heat and acidity to cut through the rich fats in this dressing so you can taste the fresh herbal flavors.

SURPRISE!

Surprise! Ranch dressing—that gloppy coating used to obscure the questionable flavor of the shelf-life-stabilized Romaine hearts in your grocery store—was originally developed at a ranch in Santa Barbara, California to show off garden-fresh herbs and greens. It was a beautiful dressing.

Surprise! In the first two steps of this recipe, I tricked you into making homemade mayonnaise. Yes, it's really that easy. You'll never eat store-bought again. Mix some tarragon or curry powder into the extra mayonnaise for an incredible summer chicken salad.

One batch and it will come as no surprise that you'll be dressing salads with homemade Ranch all summer long. Try it with fresh strongly-flavored lettuces like garden-fresh Oakleaf, Butterhead and Romaine, or over smoky, grilled chicken wings.

TIP: You can use a food processor or blender for the herb vinaigrette. Add the garlic, herbs, mustard and vinegar and blend. While running, drizzle in the olive oil to form a creamy dressing.

TIP: The sharp edges of larger, coarse salt crystals help tear down the garlic and herbs. Either Kosher or sea salts work well and taste great.

FRESH HERBED TOMATO SALAD

Serves 6–8

In the heat of summer, ripe, fresh, juicy tomatoes need nothing more than a bright red wine vinaigrette, roughly chopped herbs and the creamy, bite of feta to achieve perfection.

Ingredients:

4 cloves garlic, minced

2 tbs each chopped basil, parsley, chives and oregano

1 tbs chopped thyme

1 tsp Dijon mustard

⅓ cup red wine vinegar

⅔ cup olive oil—the good stuff!

5 medium tomatoes, cut in small wedges

½ cup crumbled feta cheese

Directions:

- Place the garlic in a mortar, sprinkle with coarse salt and mash into a paste.

- Add chopped basil, parsley, chives, oregano and thyme to the mortar. Pound into a paste with garlic, adding additional coarse salt if needed.

- Transfer herb paste to medium bowl, and whisk together with mustard and vinegar. Season to taste with pepper.

- While whisking, drizzle oil into vinegar mixture. This will form a creamy emulsion.

- Taste vinaigrette with a tomato wedge. Season to taste with additional vinegar or oil, salt and pepper.

- Lightly dress tomatoes with vinaigrette and toss with feta.

HEIRLOOMS

Close your eyes and imagine the first perfect, ripe tomato from your garden, the one cut into large wedges for a salad or in thick slices atop a burger. Imagine biting in as the seeds burst, running down your chin. They deliver the ideal balance of sweetness and acidity, and you've been waiting ten months for their return.

That tomato, the one that delivers firm meaty texture and that classic flavor best, is one of two heirlooms, either Purple Cherokee or Brandywine. The yellow and orange varieties like Mr. Stripey are often more tender and have less acidity, letting their sugars shine. Varieties that naturally ripen green like Zebra or Aunt Ruby's German, are more acidic, almost citrusy.

Try Mr. Stripey with the corn and tomato gazpacho (page 187), toss Aunt Ruby's Green with cubes of watermelon, fresh feta and a Sherry vinaigrette, and those Brandywine and Purple Cherokees? Cut those in thick wedges for this salad. They're perfect.

TIP: Using a waxy potato like the Yukon Gold will keep this soup from getting too thick and pasty. A starchy potato like the Russet will weigh down the chowder.

TIP: Smoky Spanish paprika adds a distinct barbecue-potato-chip-only-better flavor to the soup. Look for it in your spice aisle or with the Spanish ingredients in the international aisle, labeled "pimentón".

CORN CHOWDER

Serves 8–10

If you've called New England home in the summer, this chowder will bring a tear to your eye. From summers on the beaches of Newport, Rhode Island and the rocky coast of Maine to the farmland of the Pioneer Valley in Massachusetts, this will transport you home.

Ingredients

- 1 tbs olive oil
- ⅓ pound pancetta, diced
- 1 medium onion, diced
- ¾ pound Yukon Gold or other waxy potatoes, diced
- 2 bay leaves
- 2 cups milk
- 1 cup buttermilk
- 1 cup cream
- 5 ears raw corn, kernels removed
- 1 tbs Sherry vinegar
- ¼ cup chopped cilantro
- 1 tbs Spanish paprika

Directions:

- Warm olive oil in a 4 quart soup pot over medium heat. Add pancetta and cook until crisp. Remove pancetta and drain over paper towels. Drain fat, leaving 2 tbs in the pot.

- Return pot to heat and add onion. Cook 5 minutes until softened.

- Add potatoes and ½ cup water. Cook until water is evaporated.

- Add bay leaves, milk, buttermilk and cream. Continue to cook until potatoes are softened. Timing will depend on how finely you dice them.

- Add corn and cook for five minutes. Remove about ½ of corn and potatoes and set aside. Remove bay leaves and discard.

- Run soup and remaining solids through a food mill or processor and return to pan with the reserved whole corn and potatoes.

- Stir in vinegar, cilantro and paprika. Season to taste with salt, pepper and additional vinegar, cilantro and paprika.

TIME AND PLACE

I stood, sweating, in my Washington, DC kitchen on a night in July so humid the air conditioning couldn't keep up. Mixing together tart buttermilk, waxy potatoes and the sweetest summer corn, I created this chowder, rich and salty with rendered fat from Italian pancetta. But in my mind, as I took each bite, I was sitting on Bannister's wharf in Newport, Rhode Island at the Black Pearl.

I was ten years old, my skin bronzed and hair blonde from a week spent on the beach. My cousin Tony and I were seated at our own round table a little ways away from my parents and younger siblings, so like grown-ups. I was eating a thick bowl of chowder as I waited for the French Dip sandwich that would send salty jus running down my chin. The light breeze in the harbor carried a blend of brine and exhaust.

Food can transport us through time and distance, memory and longing, and— wherever we land—it brings us together.

A GRAND CONSPIRACY

Kids, your parents are holding out on you. They are part of a long-standing adult conspiracy to hog all of the tomatoes, zucchini, green beans and cucumbers for themselves. It is all built on one big lie—vegetables are gross.

You thought you just don't like vegetables, didn't you? However, secretly, from the first jar of mashed peas to last night's chicken nuggets, your parents have been feeding you a line, telling you that you don't like fresh veggies, that you'd rather just pick up some fast food. It's not true. Vegetables are delicious.

And I have proof. I've been doing four years of live cooking demos at Washington, DC's Eastern Market and every week, kids just like you step up to my table, pushing right past all of the adults in order to try plates of salad, Brussels sprouts, asparagus and even turnips (really!).

Last July we did a children's demo, turning veggies into junk food favorites like cantaloupe salsa, eggplant fries, and even a chocolate salad, with a dark chocolate infused balsamic vinegar. My friend Archer, who was six years old, came with his aunt to watch me cook a zucchini pizza, topped with a quick, fresh, cherry tomato sauce.

The dish takes about twenty minutes to make. The whole time, trying to prevent Archer from discovering just how good fresh summer tomatoes and zucchini taste, his aunt kept telling him that they had a busy day planned and had to leave. But Archer knew better. With his chin resting atop folded arms on the edge of my demo table, he watched me cook the entire dish, ignoring his aunt's requests, until he was served the very first taste, hot off the stove.

Kids, the next time Mom and Dad try to fool you, offering to take you out for french fries or to pop something in the microwave oven, you know what to do: stand up and demand some delicious, farm-fresh vegetables. It's your right.

(JONATHAN BARDZIK

QUICK CHERRY TOMATO SAUCE

Makes about 2 cups

I make this all summer long and serve it on everything from fresh pasta and steamed vegetables to chicken off the grill and white fish from the oven. My last batch was ready from prep to serving in under 17 minutes.

Ingredients:

1 tbs olive oil

2 cloves garlic, minced

1 tsp anchovy paste

2 pints cherry tomatoes, halved

1 tbs red wine vinegar

2 tbs chopped oregano

Directions:

- Warm oil over medium heat in a 10" skillet.

- Add garlic and sauté until fragrant, about 30 seconds.

- Stir in anchovy paste and cook 30 seconds longer.

- Add tomatoes and toss with anchovy paste and garlic.

- Increase heat to medium-high and cook until tomatoes soften. If the pan gets dry before tomatoes are soft, add ½ cup water and continue cooking.

- Deglaze pan with vinegar, stir in oregano and season to taste with salt and pepper.

TIP: I know you think you hate anchovy paste, but trust me on this one. You won't taste anything fishy or overly salty in the final dish, but it gives wonderful complexity and depth.

SIMPLE

My first cooking demonstration at Eastern Market was on the last Saturday of July, 2011. I was set up without a tent on a day so hot that I had to ice down salad bowls to keep the greens from wilting. Standing on a patch of dirt that sloped slightly downward sending vegetables rolling off the table into my audience, I managed to wrangle a pint-full of cherry tomatoes and slice them in half to prepare this quick sauce.

The dish is a perfect example of how I view farm-fresh cooking: it's just six ingredients, all used to highlight the farm or garden-fresh flavor of perfectly ripe cherry tomatoes. Oil adds a little richness, anchovy paste for depth and complexity, vinegar is bright and herbs taste green and fresh. It can be prepared quickly with no special equipment or training, just a knife and a stove.

A friend of mine recently said, "I've been watching your demonstrations and your cooking looks so simple, but it doesn't taste simple." I couldn't have said it better myself.

ZUCCHINI PIZZA

Serves 6

Zucchini, held together with eggs and cheese, forms the crust of this pizza. I top it simply with a quick cherry tomato sauce, but have fun and experiment. And let me know your favorite toppings. I'm always looking for new ideas!

Ingredients:

5 cups grated zucchini, about 2 large

4 tbs olive oil, divided

2 green onions, whites and greens chopped separately

2 cloves garlic, minced

2 tbs chopped basil

3 eggs, lightly beaten

2 cups grated sharp cheddar cheese, divided

2 cups Quick Cherry Tomato Sauce (page 175)

Directions:

- Toss zucchini with a pinch of salt to draw out water and drain in a colander or mesh sieve for 20 minutes.

- Warm 1 tbs olive oil in a 12" skillet over medium-low heat. Add whites from green onions and cook until softened, about 3 minutes.

- Add garlic and cook 1 minute longer. Remove and reserve in a large bowl.

- Squeeze water from zucchini. Add zucchini to bowl with scallions and garlic.

- Blend in 1 tbs oil, eggs and 1 cup of cheddar.

- Heat remaining 2 tbs olive oil in 12" skillet over medium heat. Turn pan to evenly coat bottom and sides.

- Add zucchini mixture to pan and spread evenly to the edges. Cover and cook until set, about 5–7 minutes.

- Top with tomato sauce and remaining cheese. Cover and cook until cheese melts.

TIP: Loosen the zucchini around the edges with a rubber spatula. This will help it release from the pan. If it doesn't want to come out don't worry, sometimes mine sticks, too. Just serve it directly from the pan.

PUTTING IT TOGETHER: DON'T TELL THE KIDS

You don't like skipping dessert or going to the dentist. No one likes doing things that are good for them, especially kids. So don't ruin this meal by telling them how many vegetables you've managed to put on the table. Just tell them that it's junk food—and that it's absolutely delicious. Then get ready to lick your own plate clean, because it is.

Zucchini Pizza with Quick Cherry Tomato Sauce
Eggplant Fries (page 179)
Grilled Chicken Wings with Ranch Dressing (page 167)
Ginger Mint Stone Fruit Salad (page 209)

EGGPLANT FRIES

Serves 6–8

Lightly fried, these eggplant wedges have a crisp panko coating giving way to a melting center. Frying makes the eggplant sweet and red pepper flakes lend just the right spicy bite.

Ingredients:

  2 eggs, lightly beaten
  2 cups panko bread crumbs
  1 tbs red pepper flakes
  ½ pound small eggplants, cut in 1" wedges
  2 cups olive oil

Directions:

- Place eggs in a pie or soup plate. Season with salt and pepper.
- Place panko bread crumbs and red pepper flakes in a food processor and pulse until fine (not dust). Remove and place in a second plate.
- Add oil to a 10" skillet over medium heat.
- Place wedges of eggplant in egg for 1 minute. Remove and shake off excess egg. Toss with bread crumbs.
- When oil is hot, add eggplant fries and cook for 1–2 minutes per side until golden brown.
- Remove fries to paper towels to drain and sprinkle with coarse sea salt.

TIP: When is the oil hot enough? Insert the end of a chopstick or wooden utensil. When it sends up bubbles, the oil is ready.

WHERE DO NEW VEGETABLES COME FROM?

Every year I see new vegetables at the farm market and my local garden center. But where do they come from? Are they the result of clandestine genetic experiments in evil corporate labs?

Nope. We've been breeding new plants the old-fashioned way for centuries. Just like people, when plants have sex, their offspring resemble both parents and sometimes exhibit new traits—like orange cauliflower. The first orange cauliflower, discovered in Canada in the 1970's, was not particularly vigorous or tasty. A researcher in New York State developed—through more natural plant sex—an orange cauliflower with bright color (fun!) that tasted great (for the win!).

Many of these new plants, like the small, sweet and relatively seedless Fairytale Eggplant I like to use for these fries, are evaluated by an organization called All America Selections. They recognize the best performers for gardens across the country, letting us know these plants will grow well at home.

SOUNDS GOOD ON PAPER

It all begins with a perfect summer day, warm and lightly breezy. The sun is low in the sky, reflecting off your sunglasses as you pull up to the bar with good friends for a cheap, watery beer that could not taste better passing over lips still salty from the ocean. The bartender promises great fish tacos and they sound like the ideal filler for a growling stomach, hungry from an afternoon spent playing in the waves.

Out they come, hot from the kitchen, and with a squeeze of fresh lime you take one in your hand, cock your head to the side, and take your first bite.

Eh…

The cabbage is dry and flavorless, the lime is too sharp and the fish is greasy. On a good day it's rubbery, on a bad day it's mush. The mayonnaise mixed with hot sauce and large stems of cilantro, lazily stuffed in, do little to add either depth or subtlety. Fortunately, the bar has more beer—enough to drown your disappointment.

But, with the first warm days of the season hope is renewed. This year, fulfill your wildest expectations of true summer love: flavorful cabbage, softened but still crisp; lightly fried fish, flakey and light; bright, citrusy tomatillo salsa and tart, rich avocado crema. This, my friends, is the perfect fresh bite on a warm afternoon.

Grab your sunglasses and ice down the beer. I'll be right over.

TACOS DE PESCADO

Serves 4–6

This looks like a lot of steps and ingredients. Let me break it down: you marinate fish for 30 minutes. Meanwhile, you throw together a quick salad dressing for the cabbage and mix avocado and lime zest together with Mexican sour cream. If you are making the tomatillo salsa from scratch (trick question, the answer is always "yes") then you throw those 5 ingredients in a food processor for 30 seconds. Et voilà (that's Spanish for . . . oh, never mind) you are ready to fry the fish and eat the best fish tacos you've ever tasted!

For marinade:

¼ cup fresh lime juice
¼ cup chopped cilantro
⅓ tsp cumin
½ jalapeño, seeded and minced
2 tbs olive oil or hot chili oil
1 pound tilapia filets,
about 2-3

For cabbage:

1 clove garlic, minced
½ tsp coriander
½ tsp cumin
¼ cup Sherry vinegar
¼ tsp Dijon mustard
½ cup good quality olive oil
6 cups shredded red cabbage

For avocado lime crema:

¼ cup avocado
½ cup Mexican crema or crème
fraîche
¼ tsp lime zest

For fried fish:

1 egg
½ cup flour
Cayenne pepper or chili powder
½ cup olive oil

For tacos:

12 6" flour tortillas
¼ cup chopped cilantro

TACOS DE PESCADO (CONTINUED)

Directions:

- Make the marinade for the fish: Whisk together lime juice, cilantro, cumin and jalapeño. Whisk in oil and season to taste with salt and pepper. Coat tilapia with marinade and refrigerate for 30 minutes.

- Make the vinaigrette for the cabbage: Sprinkle minced garlic with coarse salt and mash into paste on your cutting board using the flat edge of your knife. In a medium bowl, whisk together garlic paste with coriander, cumin, vinegar and mustard. Season to taste with salt and pepper.

- While whisking, drizzle oil into vinegar mixture to form a creamy emulsion. Dress cabbage and refrigerate for 20 minutes to wilt slightly.

- Heat oven to 300 degrees. Roll tortillas tightly in foil and warm in oven.

- Make the avocado lime crema: Mash avocado with a pinch of salt. Stir in crema and lime zest. Season to taste with additional salt and pepper.

- Prepare fish for frying: Whisk egg in a medium bowl. In another medium bowl, whisk together flour and cayenne. Season with a pinch each of salt and pepper.

- Remove fish from marinade, brush off herbs and cut into 1" pieces.

- Dip fish in egg, then flour. Shake off extra flour and place on a platter.

- Heat 2 tbs olive oil in a 12" skillet over medium heat. Fry in a single layer, without crowding, turning once. About 5 minutes total per batch. You can cut a piece in half to see if it's ready. Set fried fish on paper towels to drain.

- Layer each tortilla with cabbage, tomatillo salsa, avocado crema and top with fish and chopped cilantro. Love your life.

TIP: Pieces from the thin side of the tilapia filet will cook faster than the thicker chunks. Remove these from the heat first so all of your fish is cooked evenly.

HOMEMADE CREMA

Sometimes I really hate the internet. Why? No, it's not because every minor pimple I look up leads to a cancer diagnosis, it's because of crème fraîche and crema. Both are cultured cream products, the first from France, the second from Central and South America.

While most of the internet agrees they are different—crema is sweeter and runnier—the recipes are interchangeable. This presents two possibilities. Option 1: location—a difference in bacteria as well as diets and breeds of cattle.

Option 2: different ratio of cultured buttermilk and heavy cream. Shy of hopping a few flights, I've decided to make crème fraîche with about 4 tbs buttermilk to 1 cup cream, and use 1-2 tbs buttermilk to 1 cup cream for crema. To make at home, warm together to no higher than 90 degrees, place in a clean glass jar and top with a lid without tightening. Leave it out on your counter for 24 hours, stir and refrigerate for 24 hours longer.

If you decide to test the difference using the travel method. Please let me know.

TOMATILLO SALSA

Makes about 1 cup

I've tried them boiled and roasted, but this simple salsa using raw tomatillos is light and easy, citrusy and bright. And it takes less than a minute to make. It's tasty with chips and delicious with fish tacos.

Ingredients:

- 4–6 tomatillos, peeled, washed and quartered
- 2 cloves garlic
- ¼ cup chopped cilantro—stems and all
- ¼ cup fresh lime juice, about 1 fresh lime
- 1 jalapeño pepper

Directions:

- Place tomatillos, garlic, cilantro and lime juice in the bowl of a food processor.
- Slice jalapeño in half, and using a teaspoon (eating not measuring) remove the seeds and ribs. Roughly chop and add to food processor. Wash hands with soap and water for 30–60 seconds. Don't touch your face, anywhere, for the next 10 hours.*
- Pulse until finely chopped, but not liquefied. Add a tablespoon or two of water to thin, if needed.

*I would like to qualify this statement as hyperbole. Chile peppers aren't that dangerous, but don't rub your eyes or lick your fingers for a little while. Or you can wear gloves.

TIP: Tomatillos have a papery sheath. Peel it while holding the tomatillo under cold, running water—rinse off the sticky skin and they're ready to use.

TIP: Most of the fiery heat in jalapeños is in the seeds and white pith. Removing these leaves you with nice green bitter flavors and just the right amount of warmth.

PAPER LANTERNS

Physalis is one of my favorite genera of plants. Not aesthetically or even culinarily, but because of its family relations. *Physalis philadelphica*, also known as the tomatillo, is a close relative of *Physalis alkekengi*, those bright orange Chinese lantern plants that fill gardens and vases each fall.

"But wait," you're thinking, "isn't the tomatillo related to the tomato?" Well yes, they are both members of the nightshade, or *Solanaceae* family. However, that makes them about as similar as other *Solanaceae* including potatoes, eggplants, peppers and even the petunias in your patio pots.

Now you're thinking, "Who cares?" True, this knowledge won't impact your ability to make a great salsa. It may, however, make it more fun.

SWEET CORN TOMATO GAZPACHO

Serves 6–8

A celebration of the freshest summer vegetables you can lay your hands on! Honey brings out the sweet flavor of raw corn, while cumin and coriander give it depth.

Ingredients:

2 large tomatoes
2 ears raw corn, kernels removed
½ red onion, finely diced
¼ cup chopped cilantro
1 tbs cumin
½ tsp coriander
2 tbs honey
1 tbs white balsamic vinegar
2 tbs olive oil—the good stuff
Juice of 1 lime

Directions:

- Roughly chop 1 tomato and purée using a food mill or food processor. If using a processor, strain pulp through a sieve to remove solids.
- Finely dice second tomato and add to a medium bowl with tomato purée, corn kernels and red onion.
- Stir in cilantro, cumin, coriander, honey, vinegar and oil.
- Season to taste with lime juice, salt and pepper. Add additional honey and vinegar as needed.

SUGAR, SUGAR

As a boy, when corn was on the menu for dinner, my Dad would pull into Sapowski's Farm's dirt driveway and wait patiently for the next tractor pulling in corn from the field. He'd grab a dozen and rush home where Mom would already have a pot of water boiling. I'd husk on the back steps to keep the mess of silk out of the house and quickly bring in the ears to cook. Why?

Like all vegetables, once harvested the sugars in corn begin to turn to starch. Some vegetables, like corn and fresh peas, do this particularly quickly. Today's varieties have more stable sugars, but for the best corn, eat it no longer than two days after getting it home from the market. My Dad says so.

TIP: Using a food mill saves time. By pressing the tomato through, it leaves the tough skins and bitter, crunchy seeds behind.

TIP: If you have access to them, use a sweet, mildly acidic yellow or orange tomato like Mr. Stripey or the Pineapple tomato.

TIP: If the ribs of the chard are thicker than your pinky finger, remove them and add to the pan for 1 minute before adding the leaves.

TIP: Mexican chorizo is raw and spicy. Spanish chorizo is cured, which means it's ready to eat, and usually milder. You want raw Mexican chorizo for this recipe.

SAUTÉED CHARD WITH MEXICAN CHORIZO

Serves 6–8

Swiss chard has a wonderful affinity for cilantro. Spicy Mexican chorizo balances any bitterness from the greens and the spices and rich pork are a perfect match for chard's earthy notes. For a summer meal serve with the green rice on the next page.

Ingredients:

    1–2 tbs olive oil
    3 Mexican chorizo sausages
    1 medium onion, diced
    1 pound Swiss chard
    1 tsp Sherry vinegar
    ¼ cup chopped cilantro

Directions:

- Roll Swiss chard the long way, like a cigar, and cut into thin strips.
- Warm 1 tbs oil in a large skillet over medium heat. Remove sausage from casings and add to pan.
- Cook, crumbling sausage until browned. Remove sausage from pan with a slotted spoon leaving fat behind.
- Return pan to medium heat. Add additional 1 tbs oil if the chorizo did not produce at least 1 tbs of fat. Add onion to pan and cook until softened, about 3–5 minutes.
- Add chard to pan and cook until lightly wilted.
- Return sausage to pan to warm through.
- Remove from heat and mix in vinegar and cilantro. Season to taste with salt, pepper and additional vinegar if needed.

GOLUMBKI

Growing up, golumbki (pronounced ga-WUMP-ki) frequently graced our dinner table. Beef and rice, wrapped in cabbage leaves and baked in tomato sauce, would arrive to the table alongside bottles of ketchup and cider vinegar. Babci (my Polish grandmother) or Cioci Mary (her sister) would send them home in a casserole dish, or my Mom would wrap and bake them in our kitchen. In case of emergency, there was always a foil pan tucked away somewhere in the basement freezer.

While it wasn't the inspiration for this recipe, I couldn't help but notice the similarities between golumbki and this inside-out version of chard and chorizo served over rice. I think Babci and Cioci Mary would be proud.

Maybe I'll try it with ketchup.

GREEN RICE

Serves 6

Fresh herbs infused during cooking give this rice its green color and delicious, bright, fresh flavor. Serve under the previous recipe, Sautéed Chard with Mexican Chorizo.

Ingredients:

    1 clove garlic
    1 cup chopped mixed fresh herbs
        like cilantro, parsley and chives
    1 tbs olive oil
    1 cup rice
    2 tbs dry Sherry

Directions:

- In a mortar, pound garlic and a pinch of coarse salt into a paste. Add fresh herbs, another pinch of salt, and pound into a smooth paste.

- Warm olive oil in a 2 quart saucepan over medium-low heat. Add rice and cook 3–5 minutes until golden brown on edges.

- Add garlic-herb paste, Sherry and 2 tbs water. Cook an additional 2–3 minutes until liquid is absorbed, mellowing the flavor of the herbs.

- Add 2 cups water to pan. Cover and bring to a simmer. Turn heat to low and cook until water is absorbed, about 15 minutes.

- Turn off heat and let rest for 10 minutes.

- Fluff with a fork and serve.

TIP: You can also puree the garlic and herbs in a blender with the Sherry, salt and additional water as needed. Add to pan after browning rice and cook until liquid is absorbed. Continue with recipe adding 2 cups of water and cooking.

TIP: Browning the rice gives it a nutty flavor and a nice firmness to the individual cooked grains.

PERFECT RICE

Recently I got a call from my Mom. "Jonathan," she said, "lately, when I make rice, it's sticky and the grains are often broken."

Mom's rice was always just fine growing up, but I shared the one really good piece of rice advice that I knew: after the rice has absorbed all the water, leaving steam vents—small holes—in the surface, turn the heat off and leave the rice in the pan, covered. Ten minutes later you will find it light and fluffy, with the individual grains separating easily when you toss it with a fork.

I don't know why it works, but it's magic. Just ask my Mom.

WISDOM. I graduated from Colby College in the winter of 1996. Planning to return to Maine's perfect coast for a summer of waiting tables, I traveled home to western Massachusetts for four months with only one plan—avoid working for my father at our family's garden center, where I had worked every summer up to that point. I applied for every front-of-house job restaurant job I could find. Finally, in desperation, I submitted an application to Annie Cheatham, the owner of a small, organic garden center. She hired me immediately.

At the end of that spring, over lunch, Annie would tell me—with great care and a firm hand—that I had maturity and confidence well beyond my age. A trait that would serve me well, but, paired with the frail wisdom of youth, would also get me into trouble.

On my first day of work that February, Annie had handed me a catalog and an order form, asking me to place her spring herb order. I took it confidently,

proud that my knowledge of herbal plants transcended the common basil, chives and parsley my mother grew in her garden, to include exotic plants like lemon thyme and pineapple sage. However, upon opening the list of more than 100 different plants, I'm sure I turned white.

I spent the next three hours alone in the greenhouse, terrified my limited knowledge would be discovered. Studying the catalog, I ordered more than fifty different plants. Many of these I would be unable to correctly identify upon delivery, but quickly learned as I worked hard to sell each and every pot.

Nearly twenty years later, Ed and Gail Overdevest approached me about a line of organically produced and sustainably packaged herb and vegetable plants they were preparing to introduce to garden centers from the Mid-Atlantic north into New England. "We want you to be the culinary voice for Footprints Edibles," they said. "Inspire people with your passion for cooking and for sharing these garden-fresh ingredients with friends and family."

It's a good thing they were at the other end of a phone line. For a minute I turned as white as the day I had stood, alone, in that cold greenhouse. Then I smiled and said "yes."

I had learned Annie's lesson well. While my eyes still sparkle with confidence, twenty more years have given me the experience to back it up. They have also provided the wisdom to know that I can fill in most of the gaps with a quick taste of the ingredients, a phone call to Mom, or a few hours in the kitchen.

JONATHAN BARDZIK

CHOCOLATE MINT DAIQUIRI

Serves 4

It's so simple, but adding the flavor of Chocolate mint to this classic daiquiri gives it a whole other layer or refreshing, bright flavor. Plus, you can make this craft cocktail in batches, rather than one at a time. You've just found your new summer signature drink

Ingredients:

- 1 cup sugar
- 1 cup water
- 4–5 6" sprigs Chocolate mint plus extra for garnish
- 3 ounces fresh lime juice
- 6 ounces white rum

Directions:

- Combine sugar and water in a small sauce pan over medium-high heat. Stir until sugar dissolves and liquid is clear. Remove simple syrup from heat and add mint sprigs. Let infuse for 20 minutes.

- In a cocktail shaker filled with ice, combine 1 ounce simple syrup, lime juice and rum. Shake well. Taste and add more syrup if desired. Pour into four martini glasses and garnish with a Chocolate mint sprig.

CHOCOLATE MINT

Where do you find chocolate mint? Unfortunately, it's probably not in the produce case in your grocery store. Which leaves you with two options: first, you have a neighbor who made the classic mistake of planting mint in the ground. It has now taken over their entire garden and they are desperate to give it away. Graciously take some.

Alternatively, hit your local garden center and buy a pot. Bring it home and plant it in a bigger pot. Do not put it in the ground. It will spread and take over the world—and you will never get rid of it.

If you can't get your hands on chocolate mint, try closely-related peppermint which has the same cool menthol flavor.

TIP: When juicing citrus, roll the lime or lemon several times under the base of your palm. This breaks open the membranes inside, meaning you'll get more juice when you squeeze the fruit.

TIP: Any salad that releases water, like cucumber or fruit, will
     dilute your dressing. If you make it ahead of time, check and
     adjust the seasoning before serving.

THAI CUCUMBER SALAD

Serves 4–6

With the five Thai flavors of sweet palm sugar, spicy Bird chiles, salty fish sauce, sour lime juice and bitter fresh herbs, this is a wonderfully complex take on the classic cucumber salad that as simple to make as it is to eat.

Ingredients:

- 2 medium cucumbers, peeled and seeded
- 1 medium tomato, seeded and diced
- 1 clove garlic, minced
- ¼ cup rice wine vinegar
- 2 tbs fish sauce
- 1–2 tbs palm or maple sugar
- 2–3 tbs vegetable or grape seed oil
- 1–2 Thai Bird chiles, minced
- ½ tsp lime zest
- 1 tbs chopped mint
- ¼ cup chopped cilantro

Directions:

- Slice cucumbers in ¼" half rounds and toss with tomato in a medium bowl.

- Sprinkle minced garlic with coarse salt and mash into paste on your cutting board using the flat edge of your knife. Place in separate bowl.

- Whisk vinegar, fish sauce and sugar together with garlic paste.

- While whisking, drizzle oil into vinegar mixture. This will form a creamy emulsion.

- Whisk chiles, lime zest and herbs into dressing. Season with salt and white pepper. Taste with a piece of cucumber and season to taste with additional vinegar, fish sauce or salt.

- Toss cucumbers and tomatoes with dressing and let sit 20 minutes for flavors to develop. Check seasoning and serve.

BEACH BOUND

You're headed to the beach and by tonight you'll be eating dinner with salt on your skin and sand on your feet. After a workout in the surf, you want something fresh and filling—a summer meal accompanied only by sound of crashing waves, the perfect sunset and an ice cold beer.

Corn Chowder
(page 171)
Tacos de Pescado
(page 181)
Thai Cucumber Salad

CHURRASCO-STYLE KEBOBS WITH CHIMICHURRI

Serves 4

Chimichurri is a deceptively simple Argentinean sauce of garlic, herbs and vinegar. They serve it over their home raised beef, some of the best in the world. Why question perfection?

Ingredients:

1 tsp salt

1 tsp cumin

1 tsp Ancho chile powder

1 tsp Spanish paprika

4 cloves garlic, minced, divided

6 tbs red wine vinegar, divided

2 tbs olive oil, divided

1 pound top sirloin, cut in 2" cubes

2 small zucchini cut in ½" rounds

2 tbs each finely chopped oregano and parsley

½ onion, diced

Directions:

‣ Whisk together salt, cumin, Ancho chile powder and Spanish paprika in a medium bowl.

‣ Sprinkle 2 cloves minced garlic with coarse salt and mash into paste on your cutting board using the flat edge of your knife. Whisk into spices with 2 tbs red wine vinegar and 1 tbs olive oil. Season with black pepper. Add sirloin and toss to coat.

‣ In a medium bowl, toss together zucchini with 1 tbs olive oil. Season with salt and pepper.

‣ Make chimichurri: Place remaining 2 cloves garlic, fresh herbs and onion in the bowl of a food processor. Pulse several times. Add vinegar and pulse to bring together.

‣ Place sirloin and zucchini on skewers and grill over medium-high heat until zucchini is tender and meat is medium-rare. About 4 minutes per side, 8 minutes total.

‣ Serve kebabs with chimichurri sauce.

TIP: If using wooden skewers, soak them for an hour in water before loading them up with beef and zucchini to prevent them from burning on the grill.

SETTING A FIRE

Grilling is confusing and most of us, particularly those using charcoal, don't do it well, at least at first. The biggest moment of realization came when it dawned on me that I couldn't adjust the heat. When cooking in a stovetop, we turn the heat up and down to meet our needs. However, with a grill, it's one temperature all the time.

The solution? Set your fire under only part of the grate. I usually set it to one side. Then, if your food is well-seared, move it to the other side of the grill where it can finish cooking over indirect heat.

ENDLESS AND UNCOMPLICATED

Each summer when I was a child, we would pack up and drive to Newport, Rhode Island for two weeks. We stayed in simple beach cottages with exposed framing. The carpets were worn and the tiny kitchens outfitted with a tag sale mishmash of plates, bowls and flatware. My Babci, my Polish grandmother, and my cousin Tony, would join us for the first week.

On Friday night, before their Saturday bus ride home, we would head down to the docks and buy Styrofoam cartons full of seafood—lobsters for the adults, and fish and chips for the kids (who thought lobster was gross). But, most anticipated of all were the clam fritters. There were just enough bites of sweet clam to flavor these dinnertime donuts with oceany salt while adding a pleasant chew.

I don't know if it was a cool breeze that felt like the ocean, or a quiet night that reminded me of those two endless and uncomplicated weeks spent at the beach, but recently, a kitchen counter piled high with corn and zucchini inspired me to whisk together a batch of fritters. A quick light batter, heavy with corn and shredded zucchini was dropped by the spoonful into hot oil. When puffy and golden, they were removed to paper towels and sprinkled with salt.

Our guest that night, Hadley, said the batch made with a little curry powder tasted like a holiday. I thought that was delightful, and that's how the recipe stands.

Serve them just a little too hot, make sure they leave your fingers greasy, and, if possible, have a little sand on your feet.

TIP: I always reach for my rattiest old tea towel to squeeze the water out
of zucchini only to discover that when I really put pressure on it, the
threadbare towel splits. I'm not suggesting you grab your Mom's brand
new towels for this, but choose something with a little life left in it.

CORN & ZUCCHINI FRITTERS

Serves 8

Let's face it, these are vegetable donuts and with sweet corn, fresh zucchini and basil, and rich, bright curry powder, they are darn good!

Ingredients:

- 1 medium zucchini, grated
- 2 eggs, lightly beaten
- ¾ cup milk
- 1 tbs chopped basil
- 2 cups flour
- 3 tbs corn meal
- 1 tsp baking powder
- 1 tbs sugar
- 1 tbs curry powder
- 3 cups raw corn
- 1 Serrano chile, seeded and minced
- Vegetable oil for frying

Directions:

- Toss zucchini with a pinch of salt to draw out water and drain in a strainer for 20 minutes. Squeeze zucchini dry in a tea towel.
- In medium bowl whisk together eggs and milk. Add zucchini and basil and mix well, separating the pieces of zucchini.
- In a separate bowl, whisk together dry ingredients: flour, corn meal, baking powder, sugar, curry and a pinch of salt.
- Add corn and Serrano chile and toss to coat.
- Stir together wet and dry ingredients. Your batter should have a consistency of thick pancake batter.
- Heat 1" vegetable oil over medium-high heat until a wooden utensil placed in the oil sends up bubbles.
- Add batter in 2 tbs drops to oil and fry about 3 minutes until rich brown. Turn and cook 1 minute longer.

GETTING IT RIGHT: FRYING

Frying scares me a little bit. How do I know the oil is the right temperature? My fried food used to end up overbrowned outside but not cooked all the way through… and a little greasy. Here are three quick tips for easy, delicious frying:

1. *Is the oil hot enough? It takes 3–4 minutes over medium-medium high heat to get your oil to the right temperature. You know it's ready when you stick the end of a chopstick or wooden spoon into the oil and it sends up bubbles. If the oil is hot enough, your food will fry without absorbing too much oil.*

2. *Is the oil too hot? Try a test batch of one or two fritters. If your fritter quickly overbrowns outside and the dough is wet inside you need to do one of two things, turn down the heat slightly and/or make smaller fritters.*

3. *Let your oil reheat between batches. Frying food reduces the temperature of your oil. After removing a cooked batch, give the oil a minute or two to heat back up and retest with your chopstick.*

POTAGE CRÉCY

Serves 6

This classic soup is not named with the French translation for carrot, but for one of two towns named Crécy, who both claim a reputation for growing superior root vegetables. Whoever's carrots you use, this soup is slightly sweet, rich, summer and delicious served hot or cold.

Ingredients:

2 tbs butter
1 medium onion, diced
½ tsp turmeric
4 cups thinly sliced carrots
3 cups diced golden beets
6–8 cups vegetable stock (page 27)
3 tbs olive oil
1 tbs orange zest
Sherry vinegar

Directions:

- Melt butter over medium heat in a 4 quart soup pot. Sauté onions until soft and translucent. Add turmeric and cook 1 minute longer.

- Add carrots and beets. Sauté 7 10 minutes until golden on edges.

- Add stock and simmer approximately 30 minutes until vegetables can be mashed with a fork.

- Pass soup through the finest blade of a food mill or purée with a blender. Return to pot.

- Add olive oil and orange zest and simmer an additional 5 minutes to bring flavors together.

- Season to taste with salt, pepper and vinegar.

- Serve hot or cold.

IN FAVOR OF COLD SOUPS

Aside from the odd cup of gazpacho, cold soups seem to have largely fallen out of favor on the American menu. I blame air conditioning. Cold soup is a wonderfully refreshing start to a light summer meal on a meltingly hot day when even chewing makes you sweat.

I dream of savory, herbal bowls, pleasantly bitter-sweet with crisp cucumber. Rich vegetables like tomatoes and eggplant garnished sweetly with cold, poached shrimp or a dollop of tart crème fraîche. Then there's the fruit soup, sweet and light, thinned with wine and juice or thickened with yogurt.

As for texture, save the elegant smooth purées for fall and winter, with summer's fresh produce I want to feel a little body on my palate. Grind the soup in a food mill or pulse it in your food processor.

TIP: Golden beets have a milder, less earthy flavor than their red cousins. If you can't find golden beets, substitute 2 cups diced red beets and an additional cup of carrots.

TIP: Trouble finding the ingredients for this? Instead of
pomegranate vinegar, use ¹/₄ cup Sherry vinegar and ¹/₄ cup
pomegranate juice. Substitute 2 tbs chili powder, a pinch of
cayenne and 2 tbs tomato paste for the Harissa.

TOP SIRLOIN CHERRY TOMATO HARISSA KEBABS

Serves 6

The smoky, spicy flavor of Harissa balances with brown sugar and earthy thyme to coat rich meat and the cherry tomatoes that deliver the perfect pop of acidity.

Ingredients:

6 tbs Harissa paste

½ cup dark brown sugar

¼ cup tomato paste

¼ cup dry red wine

¼ cup pomegranate or Sherry vinegar

1 tbs cinnamon

2 tbs chopped thyme

2 tbs olive oil

1 quart cherry tomatoes

2 large green peppers cut in 2" pieces

1 ½ pounds top sirloin steak cut in 2" cubes (about 2 steaks)

Directions:

- Make marinade: Whisk together Harissa, brown sugar, tomato paste, red wine, vinegar, cinnamon, thyme and olive oil. Season to taste with salt and pepper.

- Mix together tomatoes, peppers and steak and toss to coat with marinade. Refrigerate from 8 hours to overnight.

- Load skewers with beef, tomatoes and peppers.

- Prepare a hot grill and cook over direct heat for 2–3 minutes per side, about 8–10 minutes total for medium-rare.

- While grilling, place remaining marinade and any extra tomatoes in a small saucepan and simmer until thickened.

- Brush cooked kebabs with sauce and serve.

TIP: To cube steak, cut with the grain of the meat into 2" wide strips. Then cut across the grain into 2" cubes. The grain refers to the lines of muscle you can see running through the sirloin.

MEAT ON A STICK

When I was a kid, fondue was a special family night. Mom would plug in the electric pot full of vegetable oil on the dining room table, as we grabbed for whichever long, two-tined fork was tipped in our favorite color. We cooked cubes of top sirloin in the hot fat, then dipped them into the homemade Béarnaise and burgundy sauces that Mom set out in small bowls.

I know fondue pots are a lost fashion of the 1970's, but I have so many fond memories; like the time my godmother, Aunt Ali, served cheese fondue. I spent the rest of the night throwing up (totally not her fault. It was an 8 year-old's stomach bug. And the fondue was delicious!).

Whether at the end of a fork, skewered with wood for a party or metal for the grill, meat on a stick is one of those foods—like anything smothered in cheese or made with bacon—that leaves us clamoring for more. And if your fork handles have colored tips, I'll take the blue.

GINGER MINT STONE FRUIT SALAD

Serves 6–8

This is so simple it's embarrassing. A quick ginger mint simple syrup, earthy honey and a mild splash of white balsamic vinegar for brightness turn sweet summer stone fruit into something truly special.

Ingredients:

½ cup sugar

½ cup water

2" unpeeled ginger, cut in thin rounds

¼ cup whole mint leaves, loosely packed

2 tbs honey

2 tbs white balsamic vinegar

2 peaches, thinly sliced

2 nectarines, thinly sliced

2 pluots or sweet plums, cut in wedges

Directions:

› Stir together sugar, water and ginger in a small sauce pan. Bring to a simmer and stir until sugar is dissolved. Remove from heat, add mint and steep for 10–15 minutes. Remove solids and reserve syrup.

› Whisk together honey and vinegar in a small bowl. Add 2 tbs ginger mint syrup and whisk to combine.

› In a medium bowl, toss together peaches, nectarines and pluots. Dress with syrup mixture.

› Season to taste with additional syrup for sweetness or vinegar for a burst of bright acidity.

TIP: Are your stone fruit clingstone or freestone? Clingstone pits hold strongly onto the fruit. You'll never get them out. It's easiest to cut the fruit off the pit, just like cutting a mango. Freestone pits will pop right out and make your whole day!

PUTTING IT TOGETHER: PARTY!

Summer get-togethers, joyful and raucous, fueled by music that makes you want to dance (and a cocktail or two that insures you will), deserve bold, fun, flavorful food. Fire up the grill, string up some lights and call up good friends and family. It's time for a party!

Corn & Zucchini Fritters (page 203)
Top Sirloin Cherry Tomato Harissa Kebabs (page 207)
Caponata Quinoa Salad (page 225)
Ginger Mint Stone Fruit Salad

A LITTLE AMERICAN INNOVATION

In 1961, Norman Rockwell drew an illustration for the Mass Mutual insurance company titled "Cookout." In it, mothers and children set the picnic table, while fathers hover around the grill. Nowhere can we see any food.

But just imagine, and give me your very best Family Feud guess, as to what will appear on those quintessential American plates.

Burgers, of course, and fresh corn on the cob. What's on top of those burgers? A single square of cheese, melting into the charred, smoky crevices of the beef patty. There's a plate of Iceberg lettuce available for topping, and if it's a really good day, Mom has fried up some bacon. It's an American tradition.

There's another American tradition: innovation. Maybe that's why Mr. Rockwell left the plates empty, so we could fill them in ourselves. After all, there's nothing more American than taking traditions, introducing a few changes, and making them our own.

This burger I've created, then, is not so different from the American classic. I've taken the corn off the cob and tossed it with bacon. Fresh Oakleaf stands in for Iceberg lettuce and our cheese is upgraded to an American cheddar. It's fun, delicious and a little creative. Strawberry shortcake, however, you can very kindly leave alone. It's perfect just the way it is.

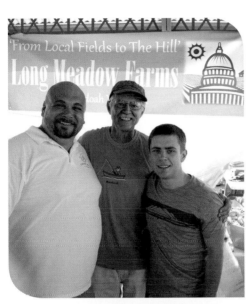

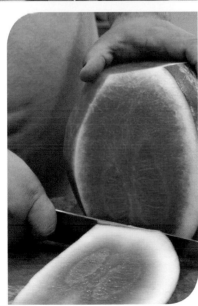

TIP: Delicious, juicy burgers need fat. Do yourself a favor and buy ground chuck that is labeled 80/20. If the second number gets any smaller your burgers will tend toward dry and tasteless. Trying to cut back on your fat? Have a salad tomorrow night.

CORN & BACON SALSA BURGER

Makes about 1 ½ cups of salsa and 6–8 burgers

The star of this show is the corn and bacon salsa—sweet, salty, spicy and fresh. Go ahead and buy some tortilla chips, you'll be snacking on this long before the burgers reach the grill.

For salsa:

- 5 slices thick cut bacon
- 1 small red onion, diced
- 1 red pepper, diced
- 1 jalapeño pepper, seeded and minced
- 2 ears corn, kernels removed
- ½ cup chopped cilantro
- 1 tsp cumin
- ½ tsp chili powder
- Sherry vinegar

For burgers:

- 2 cloves garlic, minced
- 2 eggs
- 1 cup chopped cilantro
- 2 pounds ground chuck
- ½ pound cheddar cheese, sliced
- 6-8 seeded hamburger buns or rolls
- ½ head Oakleaf lettuce

Directions:

- Make salsa: Fry bacon in a large skillet over medium heat until browned on both sides. Remove from pan and dry on paper towels. Drain bacon fat, leaving 2 tbs in pan.

- Return pan to medium heat and add red onion. Cook until softened. Add red pepper and jalapeño. Sauté 3 additional minutes.

- Add raw corn, increase heat to medium-high and cook for 3–5 minutes until edges of corn turn golden.

- Chop bacon and stir into salsa along with cilantro, cumin and chili powder. Remove from heat. Season to taste with a splash of vinegar, salt and pepper. Add additional cumin or chili powder as needed.

- Make burgers: Sprinkle minced garlic with coarse salt and mash into paste on your cutting board using the flat edge of your knife. Place garlic paste in a medium bowl with eggs and cilantro and whisk to combine.

- Add beef, season with salt and pepper and blend well using your hands. Divide into six or eight patties.

- Cook burgers on a medium-high grill to medium-rare, about 3–4 minutes per side. Top with cheese 1 minute before they are done cooking. If desired, toast buns lightly while cooking burgers.

- Load up each bun with lettuce, a burger and a heaping spoonful or two of salsa.

CORN OFF THE COB

Cutting corn off the cob can be messy. Try this simple solution. Place a small bowl upside down inside a larger bowl (see picture). Husk your corn and stand it up, on end, on the bottom of the smaller bowl. Cut down from top to bottom with a sharp knife. As long as you don't cut too quickly, the kernels will end up, nice and neat, inside the large bowl.

TIP: If you don't pit cherries often, you probably don't have a cherry pitter. I have
two solutions: either insert a chopstick in the top of the cherry and push the
pit through. Or to place the cherry on a rimmed baking sheet and press down
on it with the flat side of a chef's knife, releasing the pit. The rimmed baking
sheet is there so you can collect the juice that squirts out.

CANTALOUPE SOUP WITH CHERRY RED WINE SYRUP

Serves 6–8

Cantaloupe, its sweetness balanced by vegetal notes, makes a perfect first course soup. A rich, complex syrup of cherries and red wine makes it decadent.

Ingredients:

½ cantaloupe, cubed

1 small cucumber, peeled, seeded and diced

1 cup plain yogurt

⅛ tsp cardamom

1 tbs honey

1 tsp Amaretto

1 tbs finely chopped mint

¾ cup dry red wine

¼ cup red wine vinegar

1 cup sugar

1 cup pitted and finely chopped cherries, about 1 pint

Directions:

- Purée cantaloupe and cucumber using food mill or blender.

- Stir in yogurt, cardamom, honey, Amaretto and mint. Chill.

- Combine wine, vinegar, sugar and cherries in a 2 quart saucepan. Bring to a boil and reduce heat. Simmer, stirring occasionally, for 5 minutes. Remove liquid from pan and cool to room temperature.

- Season cantaloupe soup to taste with a pinch of salt and additional honey.

- Serve soup drizzled with cherry syrup to taste, about 1 cup soup to ¼ cup syrup.

PUTTING IT TOGETHER: SUMMER'S DOG DAYS

You're sitting in a chair, the fan unable to move the still air, leaden with humidity. Your knowledge of math and possibly your last name just melted out of your brain. There's no way you're cooking tonight. It's time for a meal served cold and, with a little planning ahead, you can just reach in the fridge, set out a few chilled platters and try and find the energy to chew.

Cantaloupe Soup
(leave the stove off and just top it with the chopped cherries)
Leftover Churrasco-style Kebabs
with Chimichurri (page 199)
Cilantro Red Onion Salsa
and Raw Corn Salad* (page 217)
*Just toss the cilantro red onion salsa with raw corn,
cut from the cob. It's a whole other dish!

TIP: Chicken thighs are dark meat and pack both more fat and
    flavor than breasts which can turn out dry on the grill. Leave
    the skin on while grilling. If you must, remove this crispy treat
    before you eat.

GRILLED CHICKEN WITH CILANTRO RED ONION SALSA

Serves 6

Where wouldn't you use this salsa? Grilled salmon, skirt steak, or pork chops. A tablespoon or two will liven up sautéed corn off the cob, steamed broccoli or summer squash. And it's perfect over rich, smoky grilled chicken thighs.

For chicken:

- ¼ cup red wine vinegar
- ¼ cup dry red wine
- ½ cup olive oil
- ¼ cup fish sauce
- ½ cup chopped cilantro
- 6 cloves minced garlic
- 10-12 bone-in, skin-on chicken thighs

For salsa:

- 1 bunch cilantro, stems removed
- 1 jalapeño, seeded, de-ribbed and minced
- 2 cloves garlic, peeled and roughly chopped
- 2 tbs minced mint
- ½ red onion finely diced
- 1 lime, juiced
- 1-3 tbs olive oil
- ¼ tsp cumin

Directions:

- Marinate chicken: Combine vinegar, wine, oil, fish sauce, cilantro and garlic. Season with salt and pepper. Place chicken in a scalable freezer bag and pour in marinade. Refrigerate and marinate for 2–4 hours.

- Make salsa: Finely chop cilantro. Combine in a small bowl with jalapeño, garlic, mint and onion. Stir in lime juice and add olive oil 1 tbs at a time until salsa comes together. You will use 1–3 tbs.

- Season to taste with salt, pepper and cumin. Add additional olive oil if the taste is too sharp.

- Grill chicken: Set a medium-hot fire. Place chicken thighs, skin side down, over direct heat. Cook until skin is seared, about 3–5 minutes. Turn and cook 3–5 minutes more. Move chicken to indirect heat, skin side down, and cook through another 5–7 minutes, about 15 minutes total.

- Serve grilled chicken thighs with cilantro salsa.

MARKET DEMO ADVENTURES: "GROSS!"

Serving up ingredients that set off an audience member's "Blech!" reflex is an occupational hazard of giving live cooking demos at farm markets. (Heck, it's a hazard anytime I cook beets at home with my husband Jason.)

My first year cooking at Washington, DC's historic Eastern Market I created this cilantro salsa, which I served on fresh tortilla chips from Canales Deli. That day my friend Seth came out to see my demo. About six chips in he approached the table, leaned in and said to me, "This is probably the right time to tell you that I hate every single ingredient in this salsa."

This happens to me a lot— usually a man, leaning across and, conspiratorially in a hushed voice, saying, "I hate Brussels sprouts/ asparagus/mushrooms, but what you just cooked was delicious!"

I love it every single time.

WATERMELON GORGONZOLA SALAD

Serves 6

Sweet watermelon, bright peppery arugula and creamy, funky bleu cheese balance perfectly in this refreshing, thirst-quenching salad that looks as beautiful as it tastes.

Ingredients:

6 cups watermelon, preferably seedless, cut in 1" cubes

2 cups baby arugula, loosely packed

1 shallot, minced

⅓ cup red wine vinegar

1 tsp honey

⅔ cups olive oil—the good stuff!

1 cup chilled, crumbled Gorgonzola cheese

Directions:

- Toss together watermelon and arugula in a large bowl.

- In a separate bowl, whisk together shallot, vinegar and honey.

- While whisking, drizzle oil into vinegar mixture. This will form a creamy emulsion.

- Stir crumbles of Gorgonzola into vinaigrette until creamy and taste with a cube of watermelon.

- Season to taste with additional salt, pepper, vinegar or oil and lightly dress watermelon and arugula.

TIP: If making this ahead, keep the watermelon separate. It will release water, which will dilute your dressing and wilt the arugula. Combine the arugula and watermelon and dress right before serving.

FINE ART FRUIT

The first cookbook I ever bought with my own money is titled **The Fine Art of Garnishing.** *It came with five small tools that enabled me to turn a radish into a rose, an apple into a bird, and, most importantly, carve a watermelon. For one summer cookout after another, I carved watermelons into serving dishes for fruit salad. Family photos reveal them carefully crafted to resemble whales, Viking ships, and baskets.*

Back then, we'd scoop out the watermelons using a melon baller and toss the fruit with cantaloupe, honeydew, peaches and berries. Today, while I still love a good fruit salad, there are meals when I want my watermelon dressed a little more elegantly. The savory flavors of bright vinegar, peppery greens and sharp cheese balance delightfully with sugary fruits. The resulting salad is a perfect companion to anything smoky and charred from the grill.

I suppose, if you're going to use such sophisticated ingredients, you should probably present them more formally. May I suggest inside a watermelon?

POACHED PEACHES & NECTARINES

Serves 6, decadently!

Whole spices bring exotic flavor to sweet summer fruit. Serve this decadent sauce over grilled pork boldly spiced with chile and cumin or spoon it over chilled bowls of homemade vanilla ice cream.

Ingredients:

- 1 cup sugar
- 1 cup water
- 2 star anise
- 3 whole cardamom pods
- 1 cinnamon stick
- 2 white peaches, in thick slices
- 2 white nectarines, in thick slices
- Half a lemon

Directions:

- Combine sugar, water, star anise, cardamom pods and cinnamon stick in a 10" skillet over medium-high heat. Stir until sugar is dissolved.
- Simmer until liquid is reduce by half.
- Add peaches and nectarines. The fruit will release a lot of water as it cooks.
- Continue cooking until the sauce begins to turn caramel brown around the edges of the pan, this may take 10–15 minutes. Watch to make sure the sugar doesn't burn.
- Season to taste with a squeeze of lemon. Remove whole spices and serve.

TIP: White peaches and nectarines taste sweeter than their orange cousins, not because they contain more sugar, but because they are less acidic, letting the sugars shine through.

TIP: Can't find whole spices? Substitute $^1/_8$ teaspoon each of ground.

WHERE DO YOU GET YOUR SPICES?

So, I've got a little "spice problem." To get mine, I fly to Columbus, Ohio and visit Ben—the owner of Spices, Ltd. in the North Market. I walk out carrying a bagful in each hand. This probably isn't a realistic recommendation for most of you, so here's my advice:

A good local spice market will change your life. If there isn't one nearby, order online (Spices, Ltd. ships!). And don't dismiss the grocery store. They carry better selections all the time.

Once you've acquired your spices, make sure to use them while they're fresh. You shouldn't hold onto ground spices for more than 18 months, no matter how much you paid. Toss anything that was a leaf, like oregano or bay, after 12 months.

Just can't bring yourself to throw them away so soon? Buying whole spices improves shelf life. After 18 months toast them lightly before grinding and you'll get a whole extra year of flavor. It just may be time to buy yourself a mortar and pestle.

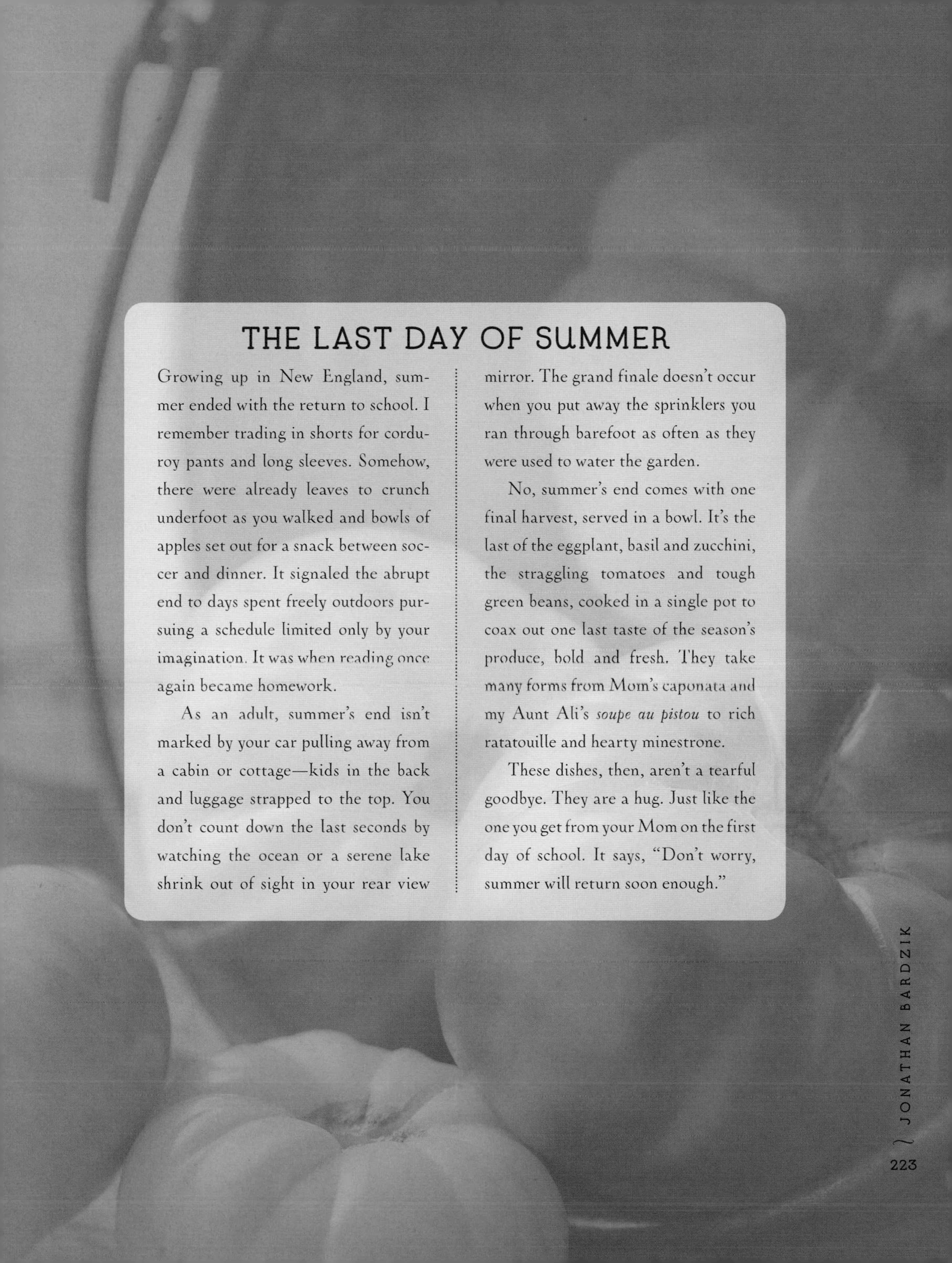

THE LAST DAY OF SUMMER

Growing up in New England, summer ended with the return to school. I remember trading in shorts for corduroy pants and long sleeves. Somehow, there were already leaves to crunch underfoot as you walked and bowls of apples set out for a snack between soccer and dinner. It signaled the abrupt end to days spent freely outdoors pursuing a schedule limited only by your imagination. It was when reading once again became homework.

As an adult, summer's end isn't marked by your car pulling away from a cabin or cottage—kids in the back and luggage strapped to the top. You don't count down the last seconds by watching the ocean or a serene lake shrink out of sight in your rear view mirror. The grand finale doesn't occur when you put away the sprinklers you ran through barefoot as often as they were used to water the garden.

No, summer's end comes with one final harvest, served in a bowl. It's the last of the eggplant, basil and zucchini, the straggling tomatoes and tough green beans, cooked in a single pot to coax out one last taste of the season's produce, bold and fresh. They take many forms from Mom's caponata and my Aunt Ali's *soupe au pistou* to rich ratatouille and hearty minestrone.

These dishes, then, aren't a tearful goodbye. They are a hug. Just like the one you get from your Mom on the first day of school. It says, "Don't worry, summer will return soon enough."

JONATHAN BARDZIK

223

TIP: Eggplant can easily stick to the pan. Using the full two
tablespoons of olive oil and browning the eggplant over
medium heat prevents sticking while reducing the heat after
browning prevents it from burning.

CAPONATA QUINOA SALAD

Serves 6–8

From summer through fall, my Mom's arrival at our home is accompanied by food, harvested fresh from her garden and put up in her freezer. It always includes rich caponata, a classic Italian blend of eggplants and peppers, tomatoes, basil and capers. This dish captures those flavors in a one-dish vegetarian homage to the end of summer.

Ingredients:

1 ½ cups red quinoa	½ red onion, thinly sliced
2 cups water	2 tbs chopped basil
3 tbs olive oil	¼ cup chopped parsley
3 small eggplants cut in ½" dice	2 cloves garlic, minced
2 medium sweet peppers, thinly sliced	⅓ cup dry red wine
3 tbs capers	1 tsp Dijon mustard
1 large tomato, diced	⅔ cups olive oil—the good stuff!

Directions:

- Rinse quinoa under running water. Place quinoa in a small saucepan with water and a pinch of salt. Cover and bring to a boil over high heat.

- Reduce heat to low and cook until water is completely absorbed leaving steam vents in the surface of the quinoa, about 15 minutes. Remove from heat and let sit, covered, for 15 minutes longer. Cool to room temperature.

- Meanwhile, warm 2 tbs oil in 12" skillet over medium heat. Cook eggplant until lightly browned on all sides, then reduce heat to medium-low and cook until fork tender. Remove from pan. Warm 1 tbs oil over medium heat and add peppers. Cook until tender, about 5 minutes.

- Add capers and cook until fragrant, 1 minute longer.

- In a large bowl, combine reserved eggplant and peppers with tomato, onion, basil and parsley.

- Sprinkle minced garlic with coarse salt and mash into paste on your cutting board using the flat edge of your knife.

- Whisk together garlic, vinegar and mustard. Drizzle oil into vinegar, while whisking, to form a creamy emulsion.

- Dress salad and serve over quinoa.

EVERYTHING YOU WANTED TO KNOW ABOUT QUINOA

Well, not everything. Just three important facts and a personal opinion.

Fact 1: Quinoa is really good for you. It's a high-protein grain with many essential amino acids. Some scientists think it's a complete vegetable protein, others think it just comes close. Either way, it's got lots of nutritional value.

Fact 2: Quinoa grains have a bitter coating containing compounds called saponins. That's good for keeping bugs away but no so much fun on the dinner table. That's why you rinse your quinoa several times. Most quinoa has been pre-rinsed, but do it anyways, just to be safe.

Fact 3: Every recipe I've seen is a big lie. The water to quinoa ratio of 2:1, leaves me with a pot full of water, even after cooking twice as long. I've found 1 ½ cups water to 1 cup quinoa is about perfect.

Opinion: Quinoa is available in white, red and black. Red is my favorite. The flavor is richer, less bitter, and the grains are firmer, more separate. If you can't find red, use white. It's still delicious.

CURRIED ZUCCHINI RED PEPPER SOUP

Serves 6

I made this soup one night after filming a cooking video. We were all hungry so I reached in my vegetable drawer for some late summer produce and this is what popped out. It was so good I made it again that weekend at the Market.

Ingredients:

1 tbs olive oil

1 medium onion, diced

1–2 cloves garlic, minced

2 medium-large zucchini, about 4–5 cups diced

1 large red pepper, diced

3 cups vegetable or chicken stock (pages 27 and 29)

2 sprigs thyme

1–2 tsp curry powder

Sherry vinegar

1 tbs butter

2–3 tbs cream

Directions:

- Warm olive oil in a 4 quart saucepan set over medium heat. Add onion and sauté until softened, about 3–4 minutes.

- Add garlic and cook additional 30 seconds until fragrant.

- Add zucchini and pepper. Cook, stirring frequently, until liquid evaporates and vegetables begin to soften.

- Stir stock into vegetables, add thyme sprigs. Cover and cook until vegetables are soft enough to mash with a fork, about 15 minutes.

- Process soup in a food mill or with an immersion blender or food processor and return to pot.

- Season to taste with curry powder, a splash of vinegar, butter and cream. A little bite of heat is nice in this soup. Add a pinch of cayenne pepper if needed.

TIP: There are lots of different curry powders out there. If you have a spice vendor you trust, ask them about specific blends. Otherwise, grab something off the shelf and give it a try. After all, it's just cooking!

PUTTING IT TOGETHER: THE END OF SUMMER

Vacations are over and you're back in your daily routine with kids at school and new projects ramping up at work. With the first frost predicted, you clean the last remaining squash and eggplant, tomatoes and fresh basil from the garden. You won't taste these veggies fresh for another 10 months. Savor every last bite.

Curried Zucchini Red Pepper Soup
Caponata Quinoa Salad
(page 225)
Garden Fresh Lettuce
with Tomato Vinaigrette (page 147)

TIP: Lacinato kale has long narrow leaves with unruffled edges.
It is mild tasting and less bitter than most other kale, and is
my favorite for this recipe. I substitute freely when it's not
available.

MINESTRONE PASTA

Serves 6–8

A late summer harvest in a plateful of pasta with lots of grated Parmesan cheese. Vinegar and fresh basil keep end-of-season produce tasting fresh and bright. One taste and you'll be making this a lot earlier next year.

Ingredients:

3 tbs olive oil

1 large onion, diced

1 large clove garlic, minced

2 bay leaves

1 large zucchini, quartered and thinly sliced

½ pound Lacinato kale, cut in thin strips

3 large tomatoes, diced

1 small eggplant cut in ½" dice

½ pound pasta, like macaroni

1 tbs red wine vinegar

¼ cup chopped basil

2 tbs minced chives

Freshly-grated Parmesan cheese

Directions:

- Warm 2 tbs olive oil over medium heat. Add onion and cook until softened, about 5 minutes. Add garlic and bay leaves. Cook 1 minute longer until fragrant.

- Add zucchini and cook additional 5 minutes. Add kale, tomatoes and eggplant. Cook until softened, about 5 minutes longer.

- Meanwhile, cook pasta in salted water until nearly al dente, a little firm in the middle. Drain, reserving 1 cup cooking water.

- Add pasta and reserved water to vegetables. Toss and cook until water has evaporated.

- Stir through oil, vinegar and basil.

- Season to taste with salt, pepper, Parmesan and additional oil and vinegar.

COOK PASTA LIKE THE ITALIANS

I'm no expert on Italian cooking, but I know enough to serve a great plate of pasta. It starts with the water—lots of it. I typically use an 8 quart stock pot filled ⅔ of the way. Once your water is boiling, add salt, again lots of it—about 1 tablespoon for every two quarts of water. Now add the pasta.

Your goal is to cook it al dente, or "to the tooth." That means it's still firm, but not hard, in the center. How do you achieve that? First, while your sauce or other ingredients cook, boil your pasta until it is slightly firmer than al dente, decidedly undercooked when you bite into it. Reserve a cup or two of cooking liquid then drain your pasta without rinsing it.

Add your pasta, along with the reserved cooking liquid, to your sauce. As the pasta finishes cooking, it will take in flavors from the pan, while the starches in the water will bring your sauce together nicely.

Trust me, even if you're just throwing together a pound of spaghetti with a can of tomatoes and some dusty oregano, your pasta just became a pretty respectable meal.

fall

TIP: This takes several days. Day 1: marinate pork shoulder. Day 2: braise meat and chill. Day 3: Shred pork, reduce sauce and serve. That means if you want to serve it Saturday night for dinner, you should marinate it Thursday overnight, cook it all day Friday, chilling it overnight, and shred the meat Saturday afternoon.

ASIAN PEAR PULLED PORK

Serves 6–8

The spicy, crisp Asian pears, citrusy Szechuan peppercorns, earthy soy and bright ginger flavor this fall roast. Cook it until the meat falls from the bones and lick every delicious smear of sauce from your fingers.

Ingredients:

3 Asian pears, cored and roughly chopped

3 cloves garlic

3" peeled ginger, sliced into thin rounds

4 tbs crushed Szechuan peppercorns

¾ cups Tamari soy sauce

½ cup rice wine vinegar

4 tbs sesame oil

¼ cup maple or brown sugar

1 bone-in pork shoulder, 4–6 pounds

2 tbs vegetable oil

Directions:

- Make the marinade: Add Asian pears, garlic, ginger and peppercorns to a blender with soy sauce, rice wine vinegar, sesame oil and sugar. Blend until smooth.

- Place pork shoulder in a large, sealable freezer bag or bowl and pour in the marinade. Seal or cover and refrigerate for 24 hours.

- Braise the pork: Pre-heat oven to 200 degrees. Remove pork and set aside marinade. Rinse pork shoulder and pat dry. Season with salt and pepper.

- Place a Dutch oven over medium-high heat for 2–3 minutes. Add oil and heat until shimmering. Add pork shoulder and sear on all sides, about 8–10 minutes total. Add marinade to cover pork ⅔ of the way up the sides and bring to a boil.

- Remove from heat, tightly cover pot and place in the preheated oven. Cook for 10–12 hours.

- Remove pork from oven and let cool. Keeping the pork and sauce in the Dutch oven, refrigerate for 4 hours or overnight. (The fat in the sauce will rise to the surface and congeal.) Remove pork from refrigerator and skim the fat.

- Place pork in Dutch oven over medium heat until the sauce warms, becoming liquid again. Remove pork and shred.

- Reduce the remaining braising liquid to a thick sauce. Season to taste with salt, pepper and additional vinegar or soy.

MAKES SENSE

Asian pears, with their spiced apple-pear flavor and crisp, almost impossibly juicy flesh just make sense. Combined with soy sauce, rice wine vinegar and a little sugar, they provide a sweet, tart, complex marinade and braising liquid for a tender, slow-cooked pork shoulder.

Anytime I develop a recipe I do a quick search on line to see who has gone before me and what they've learned. In this case, I discovered the entire country of Korea and **Galbi,** *a traditional dish of grilled beef ribs using a very similar marinade.*

In fact, I find that just about every flavor combination I try has been prepared before by someone else. Far from feeling defeated, it gives me confidence. Some flavors just make sense—tomatoes and basil, peaches and brandy, asparagus and egg. I like to think it's the intuition of a well-exercised palate, not a limited imagination. After all, if God didn't want you to marinate a pork shoulder in Asian pears and soy sauce, he wouldn't have made them taste so good together.

DELICATA SQUASH, SHITAKE MUSHROOM & ARUGULA SALAD

Serves 6–8

Sweet, floral Delicata squash tops peppery arugula joined with mild, earthy Shitake mushrooms and the nutty crunch of toasted pumpkin seeds.

Ingredients:

1 Delicata squash, halved, seeded and thinly sliced

2 tbs + ⅔ cup olive oil—the good stuff!

1 tbs balsamic vinegar

2 tbs butter

2 cups sliced Shitake mushrooms

1 tbs chopped thyme

¼ cup brandy

⅓ cup Sherry vinegar

1 shallot, minced

1 tbs Dijon mustard

½ pound arugula

¼ cup toasted pepitas, hulled pumpkin seeds

Directions:

- Pre-heat oven to 400 degrees.
- Drizzle Delicata squash with 2 tbs olive oil and balsamic vinegar. Season with salt and pepper and toss to coat.
- Place squash in a single layer on a baking sheet and roast for 10–15 minutes until golden brown on the edges. Reserve.
- In a 12" skillet, melt butter over medium-high heat. Add mushrooms and sauté until softened.
- Add thyme and deglaze pan with brandy. Cook until reduced. Remove from pan and reserve.
- Make vinaigrette: Whisk together Sherry vinegar, shallot and mustard. Season with salt and pepper. While whisking, drizzle oil into vinegar mixture. This will form a creamy emulsion.
- Lightly dress greens and serve topped with squash, mushrooms and pumpkin seeds.

TIP: The skin of a Delicata squash is so thin and tender that you can leave it on, forgoing peeling.

TOASTING PEPITAS

Pepitas are pumpkin seeds, usually sold hulled. They are flat, oval and army green. Look for them with seeds and nuts either with fresh produce or in the snack foods or baking aisles of your grocery store.

The delicate oils in seeds and nuts burn quickly, so cook them with caution. First, place them in a single layer in a skillet over medium-low heat. Tossing frequently, cook until fragrant and lightly browned. Pepitas will begin to pop like Rice Krispies when they are ready. Once toasted, remove nuts or seeds immediately from the pan. Even if you have a gas stove you can turn off, the residual heat in the pan will burn your nuts.

TIP: Don't skimp on the oil when browning the eggplant at the beginning—use the full 2 tablespoons and add more for the second batch. Otherwise it will stick to the pan, leaving all the good caramelization behind to burn.

EGGPLANT TOMATO SOUP

Serves 6

Enjoy your summer garden's last gasp with this hearty, complexly seasoned soup—perfect for the fall's first cool days. Its warm, rich flavors win over the harshest eggplant critics.

Ingredients:

6 cups chopped eggplant, cut in 1" dice
4 tbs olive oil, divided
1 medium onion, diced
2 cloves garlic, diced
2 tbs tomato paste
2 tbs toasted, ground cumin
1 tbs ground Aleppo pepper or other chile powder
2 large tomatoes, diced
4 cups chicken or vegetable stock (pages 29 and 27)
Sherry vinegar

Directions:

- Place eggplant on a rimmed sheet pan and sprinkle with salt. Let rest for 30 minutes to draw out water. Pat dry with paper towels and reserve.

- Warm 2 tbs olive oil in a large soup pot over medium-high heat. Add ½ of the eggplant and brown on several sides, cooking about 5–7 minutes total. Remove from pot and reserve. Repeat with remaining eggplant, adding more oil if needed.

- Return pan to stove with 1 tbs oil and add onion. Cook until it begins to brown.

- Add garlic and cook 1 minute.

- Add tomato paste, cumin and Aleppo pepper. Cook 1 minute longer.

- Add tomatoes to pan along with reserved eggplant. Cook 5 minutes to soften tomatoes.

- Add stock and simmer for 10 minutes.

- Purée with a food mill or immersion blender and season to taste with salt, pepper and vinegar.

OFF-SEASON

Some of our best days at the beach are those spent off-season after the summer crush of tourists return home. The days, still warm, give way to cool nights and friendlier locals, glad of September's reprieve. So whether the day was spent hiking, walking the beach or antiquing, enjoy the screened-in porch one more time with a warming glass of bourbon and a light sweater.

Eggplant Tomato Soup
Asian Pear Arugula Salad
with Grilled Chicken (page 259)
Crusty Sourdough Bread
with Bleu Cheese Mustard Butter
(page 301)

CALVADOS ZABAGLIONE WITH **APPLES**

Serves 4

Zabaglione (pronounced Zah-bah-YONE-ay) is an absurdly decadent
Italian whisked custard—delicious paired with anything from berries to
pears. It makes a perfect fall dessert when made with Calvados, instead
of the typical Marsala, and served over sweet glazed apples.

For zabaglione:

8 egg yolks
¾ cup sugar
⅓ cup Calvados

For apples:

2 apples, cored and thinly sliced
3 tbs butter, divided
2 tbs maple or brown sugar
⅛ tsp fresh grated nutmeg
2 tbs cup Calvados
2 tbs 25-year balsamic vinegar

Directions:

- Start the zabaglione by whisking together egg yolks, sugar and Calvados in a metal bowl placed over a saucepan filled with simmering water.

- Whisk steadily, keeping water at a simmer, until cooked through and volume doubles. About 5–7 minutes. When you lift the whisk, the custard should fall from it in thick ribbons.

- To prepare the apples, melt 2 tbs butter in large sauté pan over medium heat.

- Sauté ½ apples for five minutes. Remove from pan and reserve.

- Add additional 1 tbs butter and sauté remaining apples. Remove from pan and reserve.

- Add sugar, nutmeg, Calvados and vinegar to pan. Season with a pinch of salt and simmer until thick.

- Return apples to pan and toss to mix.

- Serve apples topped with zabaglione.

LEARNING

The first time I made Zabaglione was for
my parents. It was a disaster. The eggs,
whisked with sugar and Marsala in a metal
bowl set over water that quickly came to a
boil, scrambled long before they could form
a light, airy custard. What was supposed
to serve 6–8 barely gave the three of us a
heart-stopping taste.

I've told a similar story already in
this book. This time, instead of telling you
the right way, I want to share the most
important lesson I learned: get upset, be
confused, laugh, eat it anyway, then try
again. It's just cooking. The results almost
always taste good, if not great. But more
importantly, you tried something new, went
on an adventure and now have a great story
to tell.

Get it right next time, or the time after,
but tonight you have truly earned a gold
star just for trying.

TIP: In order to thicken, the custard needs to be whisked over gentle heat. Make sure the water in the pan doesn't heat above a simmer. (See page 101)

MAD ABOUT PUMPKIN

Insanity begins innocently. It seeps in slow and insidious. In my case it began, as one might imagine, with a pumpkin. Several actually. They were beautiful with shapes and colors ranging from long, beige, crooked necks to basketball-sized, deeply ridged, warty spheres of deep green. I brought them home by twos, then threes, until the porch steps were filled. I sprayed them with hot pepper wax to keep the squirrels off and surrounded them with potted mums.

Then four years ago it happened. Farmer Marvin Ogburn sent me home with a Hubbard squash. Blue-grey and the size of a small child, he suggested I roast it. I cut the behemoth in half and scooped out the seeds. Rubbing the cut sides with oil, I placed each enormous half on a baking sheet and roasted it in a 400 degree oven until I could pierce the shell and the flesh with a two pronged meat fork, like it was soft butter.

Once cooled, I scooped the bright orange flesh from the charred skin— sixteen cups in all. At two cups a piece, there are only so many pies you can make. Even soup gets old.

I blame my insanity on my New England upbringing. Anyone else, cooking just for themselves and their husband, would have eventually discarded the remaining pumpkin. But my New England thrift wouldn't allow such waste and I didn't yet know I could just pop it in the freezer.

Thus began an endless stream of culinary experimentation, pumpkin dumplings in a sauce of miso and vinegar were followed by gnocchi and pierogi, quesadillas with sausage, pumpkin stew with beef and steaming bowls of real pumpkin and spice oatmeal.

Lest you think there is any hope for me, I've since discovered more pumpkins: warty, sweet, mild Galeux D'Eysines, the rich, light Speckled Hound, dry Marina di Chioggia for gnocchi, and Japanese Kabocha for soups and curries. I've even mistakenly pulled pumpkin instead of puréed tomato sauce from the freezer (they are surprisingly close in color!) resulting in pumpkin pizza.

I'd offer this as a warning, but you'll have a much more delicious time just joining me.

CINDERELLA PUMPKIN DUMPLINGS

Makes about 25–30 dumplings

The mild flavor and creamy texture of this French heirloom pumpkin makes a perfect filling for quick and easy dumplings served with an earthy, sweet honey miso sauce.

For dumplings:

- 2 cups Cinderella pumpkin purée
- 1 tbs palm or brown sugar
- 2 tsp Tamari soy sauce
- ½ tsp toasted sesame oil
- ½ tsp minced fresh ginger
- ½ tsp Sherry vinegar
- 1 package gyoza or wonton skins

For sauce:

- 1 tbs hot toasted sesame oil*
- 1 tbs rice wine vinegar
- ½ tsp honey
- ½ tsp red miso paste

*Or substitute 1 tbs toasted sesame oil and 1 tbs hot sauce.

Directions:

- In a medium bowl stir together pumpkin purée with sugar, soy sauce, sesame oil, ginger and vinegar. Season to taste with a pinch of salt.
- Wet the edges of two gyoza skins or wonton wrappers. Place a scant teaspoon of filling in the middle of one wrapper.
- Cover with second wrapper with wet sides facing. Press together pushing out air. Cut around the filling with a biscuit cutter leaving ¼" of wrapper outside the filling.
- Add dumplings to boiling water to cook. Remove after 3–4 minutes, about 1 minute after they float to the surface.
- Whisk together sauce ingredients and serve over cooked dumplings.

TIP: Gyoza skins, or wrappers, are just the round version of square wonton wrappers. They are typically found in Asian markets or the refrigerated case in the produce section of your grocery store. You can use square ones if you can't find round ones.

CINDERELLA STORY

Flat and bright orange-red, the beautiful Cinderella is so-named for resembling the pumpkin that was turned into magical carriage. It is, in fact, a French heirloom known as Rouge vif D'Étampes. Although sometimes placed at early Thanksgiving dinners with the Pilgrims, this pumpkin was introduced to the United States in 1883 by the W. Atlas Burpee Seed Company. Yup, those are the same Burpee seeds you see in garden centers each spring.

It had been popular in France for fifty years before its U.S. introduction, prized for its relatively mild flavor and creamy, less fibrous flesh, which made a wonderful purée for soups. That mild vegetal flavor makes it perfect for the Asian-inspired flavors of these dumplings.

PIZZA DOUGH

Makes 2 12" pizza crusts

Homemade pizza dough requires a bit of planning, but it's easy to make and delicious! It's well worth the extra work and makes for a fun night in the kitchen with friends and family. Start the dough about two hours before you want to serve dinner.

Ingredients:

1 ½ cup warm water, divided
2 packages active dry yeast, about 2 tsp
2 tbs extra virgin olive oil
2 tsp salt
½ cup whole-wheat flour
3 ½ cups white flour

Directions:

- Stir yeast into ½ cup warm water. Let sit 10 minutes while yeast foams. Stir in remaining 1 cup water, with olive oil and salt. Stir in whole-wheat flour. Stir in remaining flour ½ cup at a time.

- Turn dough onto a lightly floured surface and knead until smooth and lightly tacky, about 6–8 minutes. If dough is sticky, knead in additional flour.

- Form dough into a ball and rub with oil. Set in bowl and cover with a towel. Let rise for 1 hour.

- Divide the risen dough into 2 pieces. Shape each into a ball and set on the counter covered with a towel. Let rise an additional 20 minutes.

- Press dough into a disk then push out from the center to form a 12" crust that is slightly thicker at the edge. Let dough rest for 10 minutes before topping.

- Top and bake on a pizza stone or baking sheet in a 500 degree oven for 7–9 minutes.

TIP: Don't be afraid of the dough when shaping it. I've never had an evenly round crust and I always tear a hole in it. Just close the hole and top the pizza. You can call the shape "rustic" and say you do it on purpose.

TOP IT

If, like me, you married a graduate of The Ohio State University, then you probably signed the same pre-nup requiring that you wear a team T-shirt on every game day in the fall. That's a lot of Saturdays between September and early January when they play the championship game Jason assures me they will be in each year. So put in your ear-plugs (OSU fans sure can shout), practice your response to "O-H" (Hint: "I-O") and get ready to make a lot of pizza. Here are some fun ways to top your homemade crust:

Season opener: *Use the last of summer's produce for homemade pesto and thin tomato slices topped with parmesan cheese.*

When we beat Michigan: *Ricotta, figs and precooked pancetta with fresh chopped thyme. (Because victory tastes so sweet.)*

Winning the championship: *Homemade tomato sauce, mozzarella cheese and pepperoni. An expected pizza for an expected outcome.*

TIP: Pizza requires a really hot oven. Set your stone in the oven
before preheating, and let it warm for at least thirty minutes.

PUMPKIN LAMB SAUSAGE PIZZA

Serves 8–10

This started as a mistake, but it turns out that pumpkin makes a delicious topping for pizza. A little whole-wheat flour in the dough adds depth to balance lamb sausage, earthy sage and rich mushrooms.

Ingredients:

1 recipe pizza dough (page 247) or two 12" premade crusts

1 tbs olive oil

4 lamb sausages

4 cups Hubbard squash or pumpkin purée

2 tbs finely chopped sage

1 tbs chopped rosemary

Nutmeg

2 cups grated cheddar cheese, divided

2 cups grated Parmesan cheese, divided

½ red onion, thinly sliced

2 cups roughly chopped Maitake mushrooms

¼ cup toasted pepitas—hulled pumpkin seeds

Directions:

- Place pizza stone in oven on a rack set in the middle and heat to 500 degrees.

- Warm olive oil in a 10" skillet over medium-high heat. Add sausages and cook for 5–6 minutes, browning on all sides. Remove from heat and slice thinly.

- In a bowl, combine pumpkin with sage and rosemary. Season to taste with a pinch of nutmeg, salt and pepper.

- Press 1 ball of dough into a disk then push out from the center to form a 12" crust that is slightly thicker at the edge. Place on a pizza peel that is lightly dusted with flour or cornmeal. Let rise for 10 minutes before topping.

- Top crust with half of pumpkin mixture. Next add ½ cup each Parmesan and cheddar. Top cheese with pieces of sliced onion, cooked sausage, Maitake mushroom and 2 tbs pumpkin seeds.

- Finish assembling pizza by topping with another ½ cup each Parmesan and cheddar.

- Slide pizza into oven and cook for 7–9 minutes, until crust is brown in spots on edges.

HAPPY ACCIDENTS

My husband Jason and I unquestioningly agree that when we order in dinner, we spend too much money, eat too much food and the quality does, at best, a mediocre job of satisfying our cravings. So, one night in March (having yet again sworn off take-out) we found ourselves in the kitchen making pizza. As the dough rose, I took from the freezer the one remaining container of last summer's homemade tomato sauce.

The tomato sauce we put up is relatively fresh and quick, cooking in less than 45 minutes. Once puréed, it turns a beautiful shade of red-orange. Similar, it turns out, to puréed Galeux d'Eysine pumpkin. A fact we discovered only after spreading it thickly on our pizza crusts and loading them up with cured meats and cheese.

And that, my friends, is how pumpkin pizza was born. It was a happy and delicious accident.

PUMPKIN SPICE OATMEAL

Serves 4

This is real pumpkin spice—rich pumpkin, just enough sugar to bring out its natural sweetness, and a magical blend of spices. It's almost good enough to give up pumpkin pancakes for. Almost.

Ingredients:

- 1 cup fresh pumpkin purée
- 1 cup oatmeal
- 3 tbs maple or brown sugar
- ½ tsp cinnamon
- ⅛ tsp ground ginger
- ⅛ tsp freshly grated nutmeg
- ⅛ tsp ground cloves
- ⅛ tsp ground all spice
- Pinch of salt
- 3 cups water

Directions:

- Mix together all ingredients in a small saucepan.
- Bring to a simmer over medium-high heat. Reduce to medium-low and stir as oatmeal thickens.
- Cook to desired thickness and serve hot.

TIP: Some spices lose flavor quickly after they are grated or ground. Nutmeg is one of those. Always used in small quantities, it's well worth buying whole nutmeg and grating it fresh. Keep a small microplane grater on hand for the task.

PUTTING THE PUMPKIN BACK IN PUMPKIN SPICE

I got riled up the other day. This rarely happens… I am typically pretty happy-go-lucky, but Facebook took me over the edge.

It wasn't political statements, first-world problems or one of the uglier -isms. No, in a world where we increasingly vilify real food in favor of weird, processed and extracted things, I finally hit my wall at this autumn onslaught of "pumpkin spice".

The lattes, scones and pancakes are delicious, I'm sure, but they owe their flavor to pumpkin as much as a green Jolly Rancher gains its tart, sweet bite from apple juice. Rather than stew, I stood up and entered the kitchen, pulling a container of freshly roasted Galeux d'Eysines pumpkin out of the fridge. I combined it with oatmeal and baking spices, two tablespoons of maple sugar and a pinch of salt.

And…? Success! Pumpkin spice that tasted like pumpkin. More importantly, it was hearty and delicious, the perfect start to a crisp fall or brisk winter day. You could even enjoy it with a latte.

251

TIP: In the first step, your eggplant and peppers should come out of the pan undercooked. They will continue to soften while you cook the pumpkin and finish at just the right texture when simmered with the other ingredients.

PUMPKIN CURRY

Serves 6

Inspired by the unforgettable pumpkin curry at Washington, DC's Thai X-ing restaurant, I grabbed a rich, sweet Japanese Kabocha squash and created a quick at-home version that tastes wonderfully bright, fresh and complex.

Ingredients:

4 tbs peanut or vegetable oil, divided
1 Thai eggplant or small Italian eggplant, cubed
1 large red pepper, thinly sliced
1 onion, diced
3 cloves garlic, minced
3 tbs yellow curry paste
1 ½ cups vegetable stock (page 27)
3 kaffir lime leaves
1 Thai Bird chile, thinly sliced
6 cups Kabocha or Butternut squash peeled and cut in 2" cubes
½ can coconut milk (about 7 ounces)
1–2 tbs fish sauce
Lime juice
3–4 sprigs Thai basil

Directions:

- Warm 2 tbs of oil over medium-high heat in a 3 quart sauté pan. Add eggplant and red pepper. Cook 5 minutes until browning on edges. Remove from pan and reserve.

- Return pan to heat with remaining oil. Add onion and cook until softened. Add garlic and cook 30 seconds until fragrant. Add curry paste and cook an additional 1 minute until fragrant.

- Add vegetable stock, lime leaves, chile and squash. Partially cover and simmer for 5 minutes until squash is just fork tender.

- Return eggplant and peppers to pan. Add coconut milk and simmer 5 minutes longer.

- Season to taste with fish sauce, lime juice, salt and pepper. Serve tossed with Thai basil sprigs.

YOUR THAI PANTRY

There may be a few unfamiliar ingredients in this recipe, each of them delivering distinctly Thai flavors. If you don't have a local Asian market, they may be hard to find. I never let ingredients get in the way of a new cooking adventure. Substitute freely!

Thai eggplant: *long, skinny and thin skinned, they are less bitter with more tender flesh than their Italian cousins.*

Yellow curry paste: *You could always use red curry paste instead. But if you can't find it in the international aisle of your grocery store, consider ordering it online.*

Kaffir lime leaves: *The glossy, thick leaves have a distinct, delicate lime flavor. Substitute a teaspoon of lime zest.*

Thai Bird chile: *Intensely hot, but not strongly bitter. Use a teaspoon of minced jalapeño instead.*

Thai Basil: *Brightly spiced with a licoricey flavor, Thai basil is unmistakably—well— Thai. Purple varieties of basil are close and sweet Italian basil will always work in a pinch.*

THE DANGERS OF A COMFORTABLE CHAIR

Miss Hawks taught me English at the Bement School in 7th and 8th grades. She was a proper woman, neatly and well dressed, her hair pulled back, with glasses on the end of her nose. Class was held in the library, a small house that was moved from the Swift River Valley before it was flooded to create the Quabbin Reservoir in 1939.

Class met in the small and cozy main room. It smelled of old books and held a mismatch of seating, including one plush, green leather armchair. When the bell rang at the end of the prior class, ten of us would run as fast as we could in hopes of securing that coveted, comfortable seat.

The library, warm and inviting, was a perfect retreat in the winter—just the place for diagraming sentences or reading our weekly essay assignments out loud. The chair, however, became a calculated risk. With winter light streaming in the window, its cozy comfort lulled more than one of us to sleep, which never went over well with Miss Hawks' strict sense of propriety.

I was searching for exactly that feeling, a warm and comfortable escape from a grey cold day, when I sliced red onions and placed them in a soup pot the other night. Bright ginger and sweet carrots, both thinly sliced to cook quickly, simmered in chicken stock, before the final addition of fresh pumpkin purée, leftover from Thanksgiving. The end result was just like the chair in Miss Hawks' library. This time, however, it was perfectly alright when I dozed off after dinner.

JONATHAN BARDZIK

255

GINGER PUMPKIN SOUP

Serves 6

This soup is hearty and comforting, puréed until indulgently smooth, with just the right bright notes of ginger, cinnamon and Sherry vinegar to keep it from being dull.

Ingredients:

2 large carrots
1 tbs olive oil
1 medium onion, diced
2" ginger, peeled and minced
6 cups chicken or vegetable stock (pages 29 and 27)
2 cups cooked Hubbard squash or pumpkin
½ tsp cinnamon
Sherry vinegar
1 tbs butter
Optional: Toasted pumpkin seed oil

Directions:

- If skins look dry or beat up, peel carrots. Using the same vegetable peeler, peel them into thin ribbons.

- Warm oil over medium heat in a 4 quart saucepan. Add onion and cook 5–7 minutes until softened and translucent. Add ginger and carrots. Cook 5 minutes longer until carrot begins to soften.

- Add stock and bring to a simmer. Cook, partially covered, until carrot is soft enough to purée. Add pumpkin and cook 5 minutes longer.

- Purée soup in a blender until very smooth. Return to saucepan over medium heat. Cook through for 5 minutes to blend flavors.

- Season to taste with cinnamon, a splash of vinegar, butter, salt and pepper. Serve garnished with a few drops of toasted pumpkin seed oil.

TIP: Filling your blender more than ⅔ full of hot soup risks a nasty explosion through the top. Purée your soup in batches, as needed.

ROASTING A PUMPKIN

There's something wonderful and grand about hauling home a large blue-grey Hubbard squash or warty Galeux d'Eysine pumpkin from the farm market. But at home in your kitchen it can seem a bit daunting. The easiest way to make use of a pumpkin is to roast it.

1. *Cut the pumpkin in half or quarters depending on its size. Scoop out seed mass.*

2. *Rub interior surfaces with olive or vegetable oil, place on a baking sheet. Roast in a 400 degree oven for about one hour – until you can easily pierce the skin and the flesh with the tines of a carving fork.*

3. *Remove from oven, let cool on the baking sheet, and scoop out the tender flesh. Use fresh or freeze. I've used it with good results right up to the next season.*

Note: During roasting you may smell burning in the oven. This is likely because the pumpkin releases sugary liquid, which begins to burn on the baking sheet. Don't worry. It's not hurting the pumpkin, and after a 20 minute soak in warm water, the pan will clean up easily.

ASIAN PEAR ARUGULA SALAD

Serves 6

Crisp sweet Asian pears, clean, bright peppery arugula and a lightly tart balsamic vinaigrette combine in a perfect fall salad. Top with grilled chicken or Chinese 5 Spice rubbed steak and make it a meal.

For salad:

- ½ pound arugula
- 1 Asian pear, thinly sliced
- ¼ cup crumbled goat cheese

For dressing:

- 1 shallot, minced
- ⅓ cup balsamic vinegar
- 1 tsp Dijon mustard
- 2 tbs chopped chives and parsley
- ½ cup olive oil—the good stuff!

Directions:

- Make dressing: Whisk together shallot, vinegar, mustard and herbs with a pinch of salt and a grind or three of pepper.
- While whisking, drizzle oil into vinegar mixture. This will form a creamy emulsion.
- Check balance of oil and vinegar by tasting with a leaf of arugula and slice of Asian pear.
- Lightly dress arugula and pears in separate bowls.
- Serve arugula topped with pears and crumbled goat cheese.

TIP: Dressing your fruit and greens in separate bowls makes it easier to divide them evenly or plate the salad for a party. When tossed together, the fruit ends up buried in the bottom of the bowl.

BALANCE

What are you tasting for when you try a bite of your vinaigrette with a leaf or two of greens? Balance.

Bright, peppery baby arugula can handle bolder flavors and bright acidity. A sharp, garlicky, Champagne vinaigrette is lovely—unless you are adding fruit, which generally tastes better with shallot. Sweet, mild baby spinach has a delicate flavor and plays better with mild vinegars like Sherry or balsamic. It is quickly overpowered by bold, complex red wine vinegar. Mesclun greens and lettuces are pleasantly bitter and balance best with a dressing that has a little more fat—a softer, more buttery flavor of olive oil.

However, at the end of the day, you'll never really mess it up. Taste it, adjust it, experiment with the endless fun selection of oils and vinegars and serve it proudly. It's just cooking.

JANE FORGIEL, THIS ONE'S FOR YOU

Jane Forgiel is my Mom's mom, my grandmother. She grew up in Maryland. While working as a nurse, Gram met my grandfather, a young doctor, and moved with him to Rhode Island, where she raised seven children. Unlike the Polish recipes of my other three grandparents, the dishes Gram was best known for had a context best described as Americana. They were, however, no less integral to my growing up.

Fall was marked by the arrival of Gram's apple crisp and Indian pudding hot from the oven. Thanksgiving and Christmas are incomplete without Gram's stuffing, just as summer holidays require a baked ham and baked beans. If there is one dish that truly transcends family memory, though, it's Gram's braised red cabbage.

In the fall of 2007, my future husband and our roommates decided to throw an Oktoberfest party. Heather and Mike procured the sausages, pretzels and imported mustards and made mounds of homemade German potato salad. I offered to braise some red cabbage.

I called Mom for the recipe, shredded a head or three of cabbage, cooked it until tender with red onions, cider and cloves, and placed it in a foil pan on the buffet. That's when it happened.

People began to approach me. First one, then another, then as couples: "This is delicious!" they exclaimed. "The best braised cabbage we've ever had." Of course it's delicious, I thought, that's why I made it. But the best? I had no other point of reference.

But now, year after year, party after party, I figure all these people can't be wrong. So here's her recipe, simple and delicious. If you would, give Jane a little mental high-five when you make it. And enjoy!

TIP: You're going to look in the pot at the beginning and think you should add more cider, but as the cabbage cooks, it will release plenty of moisture. Reduce the heat and add extra cider ¹/₂ cup at a time if the pot gets dry on the bottom.

GRAM'S RED CABBAGE
WITH BEER BRAISED BRATS

Serves 6–8

Gram probably didn't have star anise and cardamom pods in her pantry, but I bet today she would. She seemed cool like that. If you want to, count the whole spices as you put them in so you can pull them out later. Otherwise, just warn your diners.

Ingredients:

1 tbs butter

1 medium red onion, thinly sliced

1 diced medium apple like Stayman, Braeburn or Cortland

1 star anise

3 whole cloves

3 cardamom pods

½ red cabbage, thinly sliced, about 6 cups

½ cup apple cider vinegar

1 ½ cups apple cider

1 tbs olive oil

6–8 bratwurst

1 bottle brown ale

Directions:

- Melt butter in an 8 quart stock pot over medium heat. Add onion and sauté until soft, about 3–5 minutes.

- Add apple and spices and cook 2–3 minutes.

- Add cabbage and cook 5 minutes, stirring frequently, until it begins to soften.

- Add vinegar and cider. Cover and simmer until cabbage is soft, about 10–15 minutes.

- Remove lid and cook until most of the cider has evaporated.

- Season to taste with salt, pepper and additional cider vinegar.

- Meanwhile, warm olive oil in a 12" skillet over medium-high heat. Add bratwurst and brown on both sides, about 4 minutes total.

- Add beer, cover, and simmer 5–7 minutes until cooked through.

- Serve bratwurst over braised cabbage.

PUTTING IT TOGETHER: APPLE PICKING

It begins on a crisp morning with hot coffee, cider donuts and a car loaded with family or good friends. By mid-morning the sun has warmed the orchard and you doff your sweater, enjoying the musky smell of crisp apples and falling leaves. Back home you celebrate the fall harvest. Cider mulls on the stove, apple crisp bakes in the oven and a fire crackles in the hearth. Today was a magical day.

Asian Pear Arugula Salad (page 259)
Stuffed Pork Loin Roast (page 289)
Gram's Red Cabbage
Cider Glazed Delicata Squash
(page 265)

CIDER GLAZED DELICATA SQUASH

Serves 8

Tender Delicata squash braises quickly in tart cider to finish with a sweet glaze grounded by earthy thyme and bright Sherry vinegar.

Ingredients:

1 tbs olive oil

1 Delicata squash, halved, seeded and thinly sliced

1 clove garlic, minced

2 cups apple cider

1 tbs butter

3 sprigs thyme

Sherry vinegar

Nutmeg

1–2 tbs chopped parsley

Directions:

- Heat oil in a sauté pan over medium heat. Add squash and cook for 3–5 minutes, until edges begin to brown.

- Reduce heat to medium-low, add garlic and cook for 1 minute longer.

- Add cider, butter and thyme. Cook until cider reduces to a thick glaze and squash can be pierced easily with a fork.

- Season to taste with salt, pepper, vinegar, nutmeg. Sprinkle with chopped parsley.

TIP: Delicata squash is tender and quick cooking. It should be perfect by the time the cider is reduced. If extra cooking time is needed, add cider ½ cup at a time.

WE NEED TO GET OUT MORE

Several years ago, in the fall, I traveled to western Massachusetts to visit my family. On our way home from the airport, we stopped by Red Fire Farm. Intrigued by their display of squash, it occurred to me for the first time, that maybe they don't all taste the same. We brought four home—Buttercup, Ambercup, Delicata and Sweet Dumpling—roasted them with thyme and olive oil and did a blind taste test. Delicata was our clear favorite: sweet, mild, firm and smooth textured. It is also the perfect squash for this recipe.

How good is it? I made a batch recently for guests. Before dinner our friend Gerry pulled me aside and said, "Don't be offended if I skip the squash. You don't want me to eat it. Squash literally sets off my gag reflex." I agreed that he should skip it.

However, after dinner, with a glint in his eye, Gerry said, "I admit it. I tried a bite. And it was delicious!" I was glad. Throwing up at the table would have really killed the mood.

IN SPITE OF MY HUSBAND

My husband Jason says that beets—sweet, rich, delicious beets—taste like dirt. My Dad says they're poisonous. Nancy, my Director of Operations and Baking, tells me that her Mom says they taste like sticking your tongue in sand—sand that doesn't taste very good.

I've tried to get them to like them, serving sugary, earthy beets balanced with sharp mustard and rich crème fraîche. I've offered them up in a consommé, a bowl of clear, bright ruby broth to begin Christmas dinner. Even sweet, mild golden beets, pureed with apples have failed.

Yet, on a cool fall night, the crisp air biting with each inhalation through my nostrils, I wanted beets—real, hearty, Eastern European beets, rough around the edges with fresh, grassy herbs and the musty, sweet flavor of caraway.

I sautéed thick, fatty bacon, and cooked onion, thyme and caraway in the rendered drippings to infuse a rich stock. I simmered roughly diced beets and carrots in the broth before finishing it with a splash of bright vinegar.

The result was exactly what I wanted. Large chunks of hearty root vegetables in a thin, rich broth.

If you're waiting for the big reveal, the moment where I convert naysayers to the true joy of the beet, I'm afraid you're going to be disappointed. I didn't even bother to fill a bowl for Jason, I've never made it for my Dad, and won't send any home with Nancy for her Mom.

As kids we are subject to the flavor preferences and culinary whims of our parents. However, as adults we can eat whatever we want. And sometimes, despite your husband, your Dad, or your dear friend's Mom, that means making yourself a big, hearty, steaming bowl of beet soup.

TIP: The tough skins of beets require peeling. Carrots, however, depend on the
condition of the skins. If the carrots look fresh, tender and bright, don't
bother. If the skins look dry, rough or bruised, then it's worth the time to
peel them.

HEARTY BEET SOUP

Serves 6–8

This is Slavic: bold and earthy, a little rough around the edges; large chunks of beet served in a both flavored with smoky bacon and musty caraway. And, oh my gosh, is it delicious.

Ingredients:

3 slices thick-cut bacon

2 medium onions, diced, divided

4 sprigs thyme

2 bay leaves

8 cups vegetable stock (page 27)

2 tbs olive oil

1 tbs caraway seeds

2 tbs red miso paste

1 large carrot, finely diced

4 large beets, peeled and cut in a ½" dice

Cider vinegar

Butter

Directions:

- Sauté bacon in a 6 quart stock pot. Remove bacon from pot, drain on paper towels. Roughly chop cooled bacon and reserve.

- Add one onion to bacon fat and cook until softened, 5–6 minutes. Add stock, thyme springs and bay leaves. Simmer for 20 minutes.

- Meanwhile, in a 4 quart soup pot, warm olive oil over medium heat. Add remaining onion and cook until softened, 5–6 minutes. Add caraway and cook for 1 minute, until fragrant.

- Add miso paste and cook 1 minute until fragrant.

- Add carrot and beet and cook for 5–6 minutes.

- Strain solids from stock. Add 6 cups of stock to the pot with the beets and carrots. Stir in chopped bacon. Simmer until vegetables are very soft, easily sliced with a knife—about 45 minutes.

- Season to taste with salt, pepper, vinegar and butter. Add additional stock if needed.

HALLOWEEN NIGHT

Whether you're spending the night at home dispensing candy to grateful ghouls or chasing your children from house to house in their mad rush to fill their bags with enough candy to last an entire year, you'll need a hearty meal. Pulled pork, a pot of soup and flavored butter can be prepared ahead of time while the sprouts steam quickly right before serving. Besides, blood-red beets, Brussels sprouts and the big bone in the middle of your pork shoulder should offer a scare to every diner. Happy Halloween!

Hearty Beet Soup
Asian Pear Pulled Pork
(page 235)
Bleu Cheese & Mustard Buttered
Brussels Sprouts
(page 301)

TIP: Searing the beef should leave lots of delicious brown caramelization on the bottom of the pot. This will all come up when you deglaze the pan with the Cognac and stock—adding rich flavor to this quick stew and making cleanup easy.

PUMPKIN & BEEF STEW

Serves 6

This rich, quick cooking stew gets layers of flavor from well-browned meat, earthy miso paste and rich Cognac.

Ingredients:

3 tbs vegetable oil, divided
1 ½ pounds lean stew beef, in 1" cubes
1 large onion, diced
2 cloves garlic, chopped
2 tbs red miso paste
¼ cup Cognac
6 cups vegetable stock (page 27)
8 cups of 1" cubes of Hubbard squash or Butternut squash
1 large carrot, finely diced
4 thyme sprigs
2 bay leaves
Sherry vinegar
1–2 tbs butter

Directions:

‣ Heat 2 tbs olive oil in a Dutch oven or heavy bottomed pot. Pat beef dry, season with salt and pepper, and brown beef in two batches. Remove beef from pot and reserve.

‣ Add remaining 1 tbs oil to pot. Add onion and cook until soft, 5–7 minutes.

‣ Add garlic and miso paste, and cook 1 minute longer until fragrant.

‣ Add Cognac and deglaze pan, scraping up brown bits while reducing liquid.

‣ Add 1 cup stock to finish deglazing pot.

‣ Add squash, carrot, thyme sprigs, bay leaves, reserved beef and remaining stock. Simmer partially covered until squash is soft, about 30–45 minutes.

‣ Remove half the squash and mash or run through a food mill. Return to pot.

‣ Season to taste with a splash of vinegar and butter. Add additional salt and pepper as needed.

‣ Cook 5 minutes longer to thicken.

PUMPKIN OR SQUASH?

I am often asked, "What is the difference between pumpkin and squash?" The answer is actually an apples and oranges—or pumpkins and squash—comparison.

Botanically, squash are the fruit of the genus Curcubita. Four species of Curcubita—maxima, moschata, mixta and pepo—produce the varieties with which we familiar. There will be a test on this later.

"Pumpkin" is a culinary term not a botanical one. We typically apply it to large, thick-walled, hollow squash with tough skins.

For me, the word "pumpkin" has romance. It celebrates a time when the successful fall harvest meant surviving winter. Unwieldy and coarse, pumpkins reconnect us with the farm and garden, reclaiming food from merely decorating the front porch. Prizing it for how it tastes not just how it looks.

So whether a blue-grey Hubbard, a warty, pale Galeux d'Eysine, an orange-red Rouge vif D'Etamps or a dark green Chioggia, I'll call it a pumpkin. Except, of course, for when I refer to it as a squash.

TURNIP POTATO LATKES

Serves 6–8

Fresh, bright, mustardy turnips and starchy potatoes form crisp cakes, tender in the center. Serve them for breakfast with runny-yolked eggs or for dinner with a thick slice of rich, sweet, fatty pork.

Ingredients:

- 1 medium onion
- 2 cloves garlic
- 1 turnip
- 2 large starchy potatoes, like Russet or Eva
- 2 eggs, lightly beaten
- ¼ cup potato starch or flour
- 3–4 tbs olive oil

Directions:

- Grate onion and garlic into a fine mesh sieve set over a bowl. Press to release excess liquid and transfer to a large bowl.

- Working quickly, grate turnip and potatoes on a box grater. Wrap grated potato and turnip in a tea towel and twist, tightening to squeeze out as much water as possible. Add dry potato and turnip to large bowl with grated onion and garlic.

- Stir eggs and potato starch into latke mixture. Season with salt and pepper.

- Warm 3–4 tbs olive oil in a 10" cast iron skillet over medium-high heat.

- Add turnip and potato to pan in mounds just larger than a golf ball. Flatten with a spatula. Fry in oil, about 4–6 minutes per side, until crisp and brown and centers are cooked through. Remove to paper towels and drain before serving.

TIP: Water is the enemy of a crisp latke. Draining the grated onion then squeezing water from the turnip and potato will result in crisp exteriors and well-cooked centers.

FLAVOR PAIRINGS

I first tried this recipe as a hashbrown. Passable at best, the sharp mustardy flavor of turnips was overpowering while my hashbrowns fell apart and were burned on the outside long before the insides cooked. Serving them at my live Eastern Market demo that weekend I repeated over and over "they're not pretty, but they taste good and would be great with a thick slab of sweet, fatty pork." By the end of the demo I had repeated this advice a dozen times.

So, at the end, when a nice young couple approached, suggesting that I shape them into latkes as their family does for Hanukkah, the words slipped out of my mouth even as I recognized my gaffe, "and, they'd be delicious with a thick slab of sweet, fatty pork."

With grace they offered, "or serve sour cream for the fat and applesauce for the sweetness."

Red in the face, I thanked them for their advice. This recipe is better for it. And, when not celebrating Jewish holidays, they still taste delicious with rich, sweet, fatty roast pork.

JUST 'CAUSE

Pay close attention, there will be a test on this later. *Brassica*, a genus of plants from the family *Brassicaceae*, is one of the world's most prolific producers of edible plants including cabbage-y favorites like Brussels sprouts, cauliflower, broccoli and kale—and cabbage of course.

It includes mustards eaten both for their leaves and for roots like the turnip and rutabaga. Asian favorites like Bok choy and Napa cabbage, and Italian rapini or broccoli rabe are all *Brassicas*. Canola, or rapeseed, is the world's third largest source of vegetable oils after palm and soybean. In Europe, most of it is used to fuel cars.

Why am I telling you this—aside from test preparation? Because it's fun, and because knowledge doesn't have to be practical to be of value.

Not to knock applied kitchen science. The Maillard reaction—the browning or caramelization of foods—produces incredible flavor and emulsions allow the creation of sauces from showy Hollandaise to a simple vinaigrette.

But life is fuller when you know the history of a local highway's namesake, or understand why silver tarnishes. Hiking is richer when you can identify wild plants, animal tracks and the composition of the stone you are climbing upon.

Shopping at the farm market on a bright, clear Saturday morning in the fall is an experience made more perfect because you can jump into the debate over the difference between pumpkins and squash. White asparagus and the tender parts of scallions and leeks take on new joy when you understand etiolation. And tonight's dinner—a stir-fry of kale, cauliflower, and Bok choy—will taste that much better because you know they are all *Brassicas*.

TIP: Your vegetables should come out of the pan slightly under-cooked. They will be perfect, still pleasantly crisp, by the time they finish cooking with the sauce at the end.

THE NERDIEST STIR-FRY EVER

Serves 6–8

Celebrate cold weather gardening with this stir-fried collection of five plants from the Brassica genus of plants. Yes, there are six ingredients in the sauce, but eyeballing the amounts you'll have it all mixed together in under a minute.

Ingredients:

    6 large Pok choy leaves, also known as Bok choy
    4 large Napa cabbage leaves
    ¼ pound kale
    5 tbs peanut or vegetable oil, divided
    2 cups cauliflower florets
    2 tbs fish sauce
    1 tbs Tamari soy sauce
    2 tbs rice wine vinegar
    1 tsp apple cider vinegar
    1 tbs palm or brown sugar
    1 tbs corn starch
    1 tsp minced fresh ginger
    White pepper

Directions:

- Separate the thick stems, or ribs, from the leaves of the Pok choy and Napa cabbage. Cut the stems into ¼" thin slices.
- Stack and roll up Pok choy leaves, just like a cigar. Slice thinly. Repeat with cabbage and kale.
- Warm 1 tbs oil over medium-high heat in a 12" skillet. Add cauliflower and cook 2–3 minutes. Remove to a large bowl.
- Return skillet to heat with 1 tbs oil. Add Pok choy and cabbage stems and stir-fry 2 minutes. Remove to bowl.
- Return skillet to heat with 2 tbs oil. Add greens and stir-fry for 2 minutes just until beginning to wilt. Remove to bowl.
- Whisk together fish sauce, soy sauce, rice and cider vinegars, sugar and starch.
- Return skillet to heat with 1 tbs oil. Add ginger and cook 1 minute. Add vegetables and warm through, 2 minutes longer. Push vegetables to the side, clearing space to add the sauce. Cook to thicken and toss with vegetables to combine.
- Season to taste with salt, white pepper and an additional splash of so or vinegar.

SYNTAX

Learning to cook Asian food was a challenge. First, there are so many ingredients, then there's the syntax.

Too many ingredients: This stir-fry has five veggies. Aside from a little bit of chopping, that's easy enough to deal with. However, the sauce raises the total number to a daunting thirteen. But wait, you've got all of the sauce ingredients on one shelf, and you can certainly eyeball a teaspoon or tablespoon. You'll have your sauce together and the bottles put back away in under a minute.

Too many steps: In western cooking we add ingredients to the pan from the slowest cooking to the fastest, building flavors as we go, the sauce often the result of everything that has come before. With Asian we cook ingredients quickly, one or two at a time. Once cooked individually they are returned to the pan to warm through. Then the sauce is added, to thicken and coat.

Once I understood this new way of cooking—this new syntax—Asian became easy. Now I make take-out at home.

BROCCOLI with PANCETTA & PARMESAN

Serves 4–6

Sweet, earthy fall broccoli with sweet, salt-cured Italian pancetta is so easy and delicious it's almost not fair. Buy enough to make more tomorrow night.

Ingredients:

1 tbs olive oil

¼ pound pancetta, cut in a ¼" dice

4 cups broccoli florets

½ tsp red pepper flakes

½ cup dry white wine

½ cup roughly grated Parmesan cheese

Directions:

- Warm 1 tbs olive oil in a 3 quart sauté pan over medium heat. Add pancetta and cook until crispy. With a slotted spoon, remove to paper towels to drain.

- Return pan, with rendered pancetta fat, to medium heat. Add broccoli and cook 2 minutes until bright green. Add pepper flakes and toss.

- Add white wine, cover pan and let broccoli steam while wine evaporates, 3–5 minutes.

- Uncover pan, toss broccoli through with pancetta and season to taste with salt and pepper.

- Remove broccoli from pan and toss through with Parmesan cheese.

PUTTING IT TOGETHER: APRÉS SOCCER

There's a special joy in fall sports, running on the grass, crisp air, sharp in your lungs, and the sting of a soccer ball slapping bare skin. Or we're cheering from the side of the field, warmed by sweaters and caps, breathing in the sweet smell of autumn's rot and Concord grapes.

It builds an appetite and back home we're ready for a family dinner, something warm and filling that we can eat at the kitchen, gathered around the table, reliving the excitement of the day.

Herb-Crusted Pork Chops
(page 57)
Broccoli with Pancetta & Parmesan
Rhetta's Cabbage & Apples
(page 291)

TIP: Watch the broccoli, being careful not to overcook. It should be bright green and the stems still crisp-tender.

CHIVE GOAT CHEESE MASHED CAULIFLOWER

Serves 4-6

We fight over every batch of this creamy cauliflower, rich with goat cheese and grounded by the grassy, oniony flavor of fresh chives, still bright in your fall garden.

Ingredients:

    6 cups cauliflower florets
    2 cloves garlic, minced
    1 cup whole milk
    4 ounces soft goat cheese
    4 tbs minced chives
    2 tbs olive oil—the good stuff!

Directions:

- Place cauliflower, garlic and milk in a small saucepan. Cover and simmer over low heat until mashably tender, about 10–12 minutes.

- Mash cauliflower and garlic. Blend in goat cheese, chives and 2 tablespoons olive oil.

- Season to taste with salt and pepper.

WHITE AS THE DRIVEN SNOW

Yup, I'm about to talk more science. But don't worry, you've got this. We're going to talk about etiolation.

Etiolation is the process of growing plants without allowing them to photosynthesize. You did this back in kindergarten when you sprouted a bean seed in a plastic bag between two damp paper towels. When you took it out to pot up, the bean sprout was white and tender.

This process is used the same way to make some foods white and tender. The next time you enjoy the white parts of leeks and scallions, nutty white asparagus, tender, mild endive or even cauliflower, grown carefully wrapped in its own leaves, thank etiolation. Your friends and family will think you're pretty cool.

TIP: Watch the temperature while steaming the cauliflower. If milk gets too hot it will boil over in the pan, making a mess of your stove-top.

BREAKING AND ENTERING FOR HORTICULTURE.

On the third weekend of October in 1997, Jessica Brewer made the four-hour drive from Boothbay Harbor, Maine to visit me in Pelham, Massachusetts. From there we drove another two hours to Stockbridge, in the Berkshires, to visit Naumkeag, the former estate of the Choate family.

Jess is a fellow plant nerd and she made the long trip to see the gardens that landscape architect Fletcher Steele designed in the mid-twentieth century for Mabel Choate. His best known work is a set of arched staircases, with white rails over blue alcoves. It is surrounded by tall, white birch underplanted with deep green yews.

We pulled up to the front gate and read the sign: "closed for the season." Open from Memorial Day to Columbus Day, we were one weekend late. Wracking my brain for a way to get in, we drove to nearby Windy Hill Farm to visit owner and farmer Dennis Mareb.

"I don't know anyone to call," he said, "but you can park in the middle of town and walk out through the cemetery. Cross the field and walk up the hill. If no one sees you, enjoy a private tour. But, before you go," he added, "pick some apples."

We departed an hour later with two bags full from Dennis' collection of more than 25 apple varieties including heirlooms ranging in size from a child's fist to a softball, and colors from golden yellow to cherry red and deep burgundy.

Back to Naumkeag. We successfully crossed the field, climbed the hill and walked up Fletcher Steele's brilliantly designed steps to the brick rill above. We marveled at the bright yellow gingko leaves falling around a low hedge of boxwood encircled by the broad, blue-green blades of German iris.

At my family's home that night, Jess turned several of Dennis's apples into a pie, quickly throwing together her crust from memory and feel. Always delicious, it was even better for the serendipity of our visit to Windy Hill, and a little bit of breaking and entering for horticulture.

Please note: Naumkeag is a wonderful historic property preserved and maintained by the Trustees of Reservations. I wholeheartedly encourage a strictly legal visit during any of their open weekends. They're even staying open later into October. I hope it wasn't me.

JONATHAN BARDZIK

ASIAN PEAR APPLESAUCE

Makes about 2 cups

The spiced notes of Asian pear with the balanced warm, bright notes of cinnamon, star anise and cloves make this applesauce an exotic, yet still comforting, treat.

Ingredients:

1 sweet apple, like Fuji or Cameo
1 tart apple, like Mutsu or Stayman
1 Asian pear
1 cinnamon stick
1 star anise
3 cloves
½ cup apple cider
Lemon juice
Honey

Directions:

- Core and roughly chop the apples and pear into 2" chunks.
- Place in a 2 quart saucepan with the cinnamon, star anise, cloves and cider.
- Simmer over medium heat for 8–12 minutes until fruit is very tender.
- Transfer contents to food mill and process. If needed, add a splash of lemon juice or drizzle of honey.

TIP: A little practice with your selection of apples will provide the right balance of sweetness and acidity, eliminating the need for lemon juice or honey.

ASIAN PEARS

I always thought of Asian pears as an exotic treat, obtained at specialty grocers, each one individually wrapped to protect its delicate skin. They offered crisp and very wet flesh with a mild flavor that combined apple and pear. Then, my first fall at Eastern Market, I tasted a locally grown Asian pear.

From the first bite, it was magic. The flesh was far more crisp with none of the graininess of the ones in the grocery store. The sweet flavor was complex and spiced. The skins came in two colors, brown and yellow, the yellow slightly sweeter and milder in flavor.

This exotic treat has become a local delight I enjoy annually. How? Asian pears grow well in the U.S., comfortable in zones 5–9—that's as far north as Massachusetts and Nebraska down to northern Florida. Can't find them at your local market? Many varieties top out under 15' in height and might be the perfect tree for your yard.

TIP: If you can, buy your bread a day ahead, cut it into cubes and leave it out overnight on a baking sheet. Stale bread makes better stuffing.

SAUSAGE APPLE MUSHROOM STUFFING

Serves 8

Earthy mushrooms, sweet apples and rich turkey sausage make a perfect stuffing for turkey, chicken or a pork loin, although that means not eating the entire batch right out of the pan!

Ingredients:

6 cups dense white bread, cut in ½" cubes

1 tbs olive oil

4 turkey sausage links

3 tbs butter

1 onion, diced

4 celery ribs, thinly sliced

2 cloves garlic, minced

4 cups chopped Crimini mushrooms

¼ cup Calvados or brandy

1 large sweet tart apple like Stayman, cut in ½" dice

2 tbs chopped thyme

1 cup vegetable or chicken stock (pages 27 and 29)

¼ cup chopped parsley

Directions:

- Toast bread in a 400 degree oven until brown and crisp.

- Warm olive oil in a 12" skillet over medium heat. Add sausages and cook until browned. Remove from pan and reserve. After resting, quarter and slice thinly.

- Return pan to heat with butter. Add onion and celery. Cook until softened.

- Add garlic and mushrooms. Cook until mushrooms are softened. Deglaze pan with Calvados.

- Add sausage, apple and thyme to pan with chopped mushrooms.

- Add bread to pan and sprinkle with all of stock. Cook, stirring infrequently, until stock is absorbed by bread and bread begins to brown on bottom of pan.

- Toss with parsley and season to taste with salt and pepper.

GETTING STUFFING JUST RIGHT

Mom always made her stuffing the night before Thanksgiving. The smell of butter—lots of butter—onions and celery filling the house started mouths watering hours before dinner was served the next day.

While Mom made it look easy, I successfully burned my stuffing for many years. Here's what I've learned from my mistakes. One, don't skimp on the butter. Once the bread gets moist, it needs lots of fat to keep from sticking. Besides, it's stuffing. It's not supposed to be light. Two, make sure your bread is stale and crisp. Otherwise all that liquid turns it soggy rather than pleasantly spongy.

Three, don't play with your food. Once you sprinkle the stock over the stuffing, give it a quick toss then let it sit for a few minutes while the stock is absorbed and the bread begins to brown. If you keep stirring it the bread never gets toasted and you end up with a thick layer of burnt mush. Fourth, who cares? Perfect or not you're still going to eat every last bite.

TIP: Stuffing will spill out of the roast while you try and roll it. The slices on the end will also be a little empty. Don't worry, it's not you. Besides, those are the slices you get to pick at "just to make sure it tastes okay."

STUFFED PORK LOIN ROAST

Serves 8–1

Sweet, juicy pork, butterflied and rolled with a sweet apple and earthy mushroom stuffing makes an elegant presentation. The taste is delicious, too.

Ingredients:

2–3 pound pork loin roast
1 recipe Sausage Apple Mushroom Stuffing (page 287)
2 tbs olive oil
3–4 ribs celery, chopped
1 onion, chopped
1 sweet-tart apple, like Stayman, chopped
¼ cup Calvados or brandy
3 cups chicken stock (page 29)
4 sprigs thyme
4 sprigs parsley
2 tbs cold butter

Directions:

- Heat oven to 350 degrees.
- Butterfly roast by slicing the long way almost all the way through, leaving one side intact. Lay flat, cover with plastic wrap and pound out to ½" thick.
- Spread stuffing over pork. Beginning on a short side, roll like a jelly roll and bind in several places with kitchen twine.
- Heat oil in roasting pan over medium-high heat. Add pork and sear on all sides, until golden brown.
- Remove pork and add celery, onions and apple to pan. Cook for 5 minutes. Deglaze with Calvados.
- Add 1 cup stock, thyme and parsley. Place pork on bed of vegetables and roast in oven until thermometer reads 140 degrees in center.
- Remove pork and let rest tented with foil.
- Strain pan juices and return to pan along with 2 remaining cups stock. Reduce to 1 ½ cups, adding any juices that accumulate under the roast.
- Remove pan from heat and whisk in cold butter. Slice pork and serve with pan sauce.

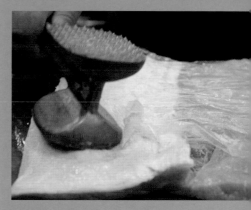

POUNDING MEAT

Pounding meat is a skill we don't use much these days, meaning it's likely you don't have a meat mallet in the house. Which is okay, you probably have other heavy objects like a wine bottle, a small skillet or a sledgehammer (I'm just kidding about the last one). Your goal is to pound the meat into an even thickness and shape. To do this, work from the center of the meat to the outside.

If you do have a meat mallet at home it likely has two sides, one with sharp spikes and the other flat. The spikes are for tenderizing tough cuts of meat. The flat side is the one you use to pound it out. I've never actually used the pointy side.

So, grab something heavy and pound away. Just think how relaxed you'll be for dinner.

RHETTA'S CABBAGE & APPLES

Serves 6

Fatty salty pork, sweet apples and rich Calvados turn ordinary white cabbage into something special. My sincere thanks to Rhetta McIff for inspiring this recipe.

Ingredients:

1 tbs olive oil
¼ pound guanciale or salt pork, diced
1 tbs mustard seed
½ medium onion, diced
4 cups shredded cabbage
2 apples, cored and thinly sliced
¼ cup Calvados
Sherry vinegar
2 tbs cream (optional)

Directions:

- In a large skillet over medium heat, lightly brown guanciale.
- Add mustard seeds and cook about 1 minute until they begin to pop.
- Add onion to pan and sauté until softened.
- Add cabbage and cook 3–5 minutes until slightly softened and edges begin to brown.
- Add apple and cook until cabbage and apples are soft, about 10–12 minutes longer.
- Pour Calvados in to the hot pan and scrape up any brown bits.
- Season to taste with salt, pepper and vinegar. Add cream and cook 30 seconds until thickened if desired.

TIP: The cream is mellow and rich, but it will cover the apple and cabbage flavors a bit. Either way is delicious!

#TESTKITCHEN

Where do all of the recipes come from for my weekly, live cooking demonstrations, blog and cookbooks? Every Tuesday night, starting around 7, my team and I gather in the kitchen to develop new recipes, an average of five each week. Each recipe begins with fresh, seasonal ingredients from the Market. Sometimes recipe ideas are pure inspiration, other times we'll pour through books and search the internet for interesting ways the ingredients have been prepared before to use as our jumping off point.

My secret to sustaining creative energy week after week, year after year, is the amazing community that has come together online. Your ideas, as you join us each week on Facebook, Instagram and Twitter, shape recipes, from an added seasoning to major direction. It was Rhetta's idea for pairing apples, pork and a touch of cream with cabbage that led me to develop this recipe. I and the many, many people who have eaten it are grateful.

PANCETTA SAUTÉED GOLDRUSH APPLES

Serves 8

Salty pancetta, sweet-tart apples and just a touch of grassy parsley lend this side a flavor that is much greater than the sum of its parts.

Ingredients:

1 tbs olive oil
½ pound of pancetta, diced
4 GoldRush, or other sweet-tart cooking apples
    cut in ¼" matchsticks
¼ cup parsley
Apple cider vinegar

Directions:

- Warm 1 tbs olive oil in a 12" skillet over medium heat. Add pancetta and cook until browned and fat is rendered.
- Remove pancetta with a slotted spoon and reserve on paper towels.
- Add apples to pan with pancetta fat, increase heat to medium-high and cook until beginning to brown, 3–4 minutes.
- Cover pan and cook 3–4 minutes until apples begin to soften.
- Remove lid and cook until apples are just fork tender.
- Season to taste with parsley, salt, pepper and vinegar.

TIP: Pancetta is salt-cured Italian bacon. It's perfect when you want clean, salty, sweet pork fat without the smoky flavor of American bacon.

OVERNIGHT SUCCESS

GoldRush (yes, that's how it's spelled) apples appeared at my local farm market two years ago and took off, an overnight success. Sort of.

The first seedling of GoldRush was planted at the Purdue University Research Farm in Lafayette, Indiana in 1973. Seven years later it was selected as showing promise. In 1993, it was released for testing at private farms around the country.

Thirty years later GoldRush experienced overnight success. This cross with Golden Delicious—typically mealy, with an insipidly sweet flavor lacking acidity—far outshines its parent. While the skin may have the same smooth, wax-free appearance, the flesh inside is wonderfully crisp, with beautifully balanced sweetness and acidity and the complex spiced notes of a Pippen.

I'm gushing but from harvest to late winter storage it will live up to my strong praise. Find some and join the breakout success.

PORK IS THE ANSWER

My husband Jason and my brother Alec are allies. Each the youngest of three, they speak a common language; one I'm not too sure I approve of. In addition to their inability to find humor in the harmless practical jokes I may have played on Alec when we were kids (pouring maple syrup in the water bottle he used for combing his hair, for instance), at Thanksgiving dinner they prefer the canned, gelatinous abomination known as cranberry sauce, over fresh, whole fruit.

I'm not a purist. My Aunt Ali's cranberry mold, set with walnuts and whole cranberries in gelatin is a sentimental favorite, served at the Thanksgiving meals of my childhood. Today, I get equal satisfaction from compotes created with Port wine, orange zest, pearl and Cipollini onions, whole spices, apples and pear. However, despite my best efforts, because of Jason and Alec, each Thanksgiving I am forced to open one solitary can in the preparation of an otherwise farm-fresh meal. Until this year.

If there is one way to win over men's palates, it's with a really fatty piece of pork. I promise, at the mere mention of pork belly, your father, brothers and uncles will gladly turn off the game and come running to the dining room table.

So this year I set out with a mission. I created a compote of whole cranberries cooked down in sweet cider with Bosc pears, and seasoned with berry-flavored pink peppercorns and piney rosemary. It was a culinary triumph, a brilliant discovery of perfectly paired flavors, but there was no way that Alec and Jason would eat it. Unless…

I rubbed a thick slab of pork belly with smoky Spanish paprika. Two days later I seared it before braising in a sweet, tart blend of apple cider, cranberry juice and cider vinegar. After six hours in the oven it was flavorful, tender and sweet. I placed the pork belly under the broiler, crisping up the fat, before layering thick slices over the pink peppercorn, cranberry compote.

Alec and Jason, this round goes to me. Now if I could only get them to eat beets…

CRANBERRY PEAR PINK PEPPERCORN COMPOTE

Makes about 2 cups compote

The berry notes in pink peppercorns lend a unique flavor to this cranberry compote sweetened with cider, pears and jam.

Ingredients:

12 ounces, about 3 cups cranberries

2 large Bosc pears, cut in a ½" dice

1 cup tart jam like cranberry, sour cherry or raspberry

1 cup apple cider

2 tbs chopped rosemary, divided

1 tbs pink peppercorns, crushed

White balsamic vinegar

Directions:

- Combine cranberries, pears, jam and cider in a 2 quart saucepan. Cover and bring to a boil over medium-high heat. Cook for 5 minutes until cranberries begin to pop and release liquid.

- Stir 1 tbs rosemary and pink peppercorns into the saucepan. Leave uncovered and continue to cook for 20–25 minutes until thickened.

- Stir in remaining tablespoon of chopped rosemary and season to taste with a splash of vinegar and a pinch of salt.

- If the compote is tarter than you'd like, add 1–2 tbs sugar or honey.

TIP: The jam in this compote adds all the sugar you should need while contributing another layer of flavor.

TARTING UP CRANBERRIES

With all due respect to my Mom's version of Gram's stuffing and Auntie's Rum Chiffon Pie, it was Aunt Ali's cranberry mold that made Thanksgiving dinner exceptional. Aunt Ali, my godmother, chopped fresh cranberries, mixed them with earthy walnuts and suspended them in gelatin, set in a Bundt pan mold. The result was tart-sweet and fresh, a welcome break from the rich vegetables, starches and gravy-slathered turkey that crowded the other ninety-five percent of our heaped plates.

One year, however, I was inspired by Renee Shields-Farr at Sapore Oil and Vinegar who asked, "Have you ever tasted a pink peppercorn?" I hadn't.

Biting in, I first tasted a mix of pear and berries that was reminiscent of sugary breakfast cereal. Then came the peppery bite. So pears and berries it was. I added jelly, rather than pure sugar, to sweeten, and rosemary for balance and depth. It's different, and it's good. Aunt Ali's though is still my favorite. Thanksgiving, after all, is a meal of family traditions.

TIP: Braising the meat longer makes it more tender.
It was delicious at 2 1/2 hours but even better at 7.

CIDER BRAISED PORK BELLY

Serves 6–8 as a side

Rich decadent pork belly is the same cut that is cured and smoked to make bacon. Dry marinated for 24 hours, slow braised then broiled, it is crisp and complex, yet still comforting.

Ingredients:

- 1 ½–2 pounds pork belly
- 1 tbs salt
- 2 tbs Spanish paprika
- 1 tbs ground Aleppo pepper (or 1 tsp cayenne)
- 1 tbs fresh-cracked black pepper
- 1 tbs olive oil
- 2 large shallots, minced
- 2 tbs red miso paste
- 1 cup apple cider
- 1 cup cranberry juice
- ½ cup Sherry
- ¼ cup apple cider vinegar
- 2 tbs maple or brown sugar
- ½ tsp whole peppercorns

Directions:

- Mix together salt, Spanish paprika, hot pepper and black pepper. Using the tip of a sharp knife, cut a cross hatch pattern into the skin side of the slab without penetrating into the meat. Rub pork belly with spice mix and refrigerate overnight, up to 24 hours.

- Warm olive oil in a Dutch oven over medium heat. Add pork belly and sear on all sides, starting with the skin side down. Remove pork belly and reserve.

- Pour off all but 2 tbs fat and return Dutch oven to medium heat. Add shallots and sauté until soft. Add miso and cook 1 minute longer. Add cider, Sherry and vinegar to pan. Bring to a boil. Add pork belly. The liquid should come half way up the slab of meat. Cover and place in 200 degree oven to braise for 2 ½ to 7 hours, until fork tender.

- Remove pork belly from braising liquid and place skin side up on a rimmed sheet pan. Set an oven rack 8-10" under the broiler. Broil pork belly 3–4 minutes, crisping up the skin. Watch carefully, making sure not to burn.

- Cut pork belly into ½" thick slices and serve over Pink Peppercorn Cranberry Compote (page 297).

PUTTING IT TOGETHER: THANKSGIVING'S NEW TRADITIONS

There are some non-negotiables for Thanksgiving dinner. My turkey is roasted with my Grandmother's bread stuffing. Mashed potatoes shouldn't be dressed up and apple pie is not an opportunity to be creative. Neither is pumpkin.

These aren't rules, but traditions. Every family has them and they are sacred. But around the edges you can play. Have fun with the sides, add a dessert or start with a soup. And if you really want to, add some truffle oil to the mashed potatoes. Please just leave a small bowl plain on the side for me.

This year's sides:

Perfect Mashed Potatoes (page 309)
Kale and Cauliflower Gratin (page 305)
Cider-braised Pork Belly with Pink Peppercorn Cranberry Compote (page 297)
Broccoli with Pancetta and Parmesan (page 279)
Rhetta's Cabbage and Apples (page 291)

BLEU CHEESE & MUSTARD BUTTERED BRUSSELS SPROUTS

Serves 6

Bleu cheese and sharp, grainy mustard pair with rich butter to top fresh, bright steamed Brussels sprouts. You'll enjoy the extra butter on a steak, over chicken, green beans, roast cauliflower...

Ingredients:

1–1 ½ pounds Brussels sprouts
½ pound butter, softened
4 ounces sharp bleu cheese, softened
2 tbs grainy mustard
1 shallot, finely minced
2 tbs minced parsley
Champagne vinegar

Directions:

- Trim bases of Brussels sprouts, cut in half and remove any loose or discolored leaves.

- Place a steamer insert into a 4 quart saucepan with 1" water and bring to a boil. Add Brussels sprouts and cook until just crisp-tender. The core should still be very firm.

- Blend together butter, bleu cheese, mustard, shallot and parsley using a spatula or food processor.

- Blend in ½ tsp vinegar a few drops at a time.

- Remove Brussels sprouts from water and toss with 3–4 tbs butter.

- Roll remaining butter in parchment or plastic wrap and freeze.

TIP: You can make the bleu cheese mustard butter ahead of time and chill it in the fridge or freezer. Steam some Brussels sprouts on that busy Tuesday after work and you're ready to eat!

SHARING THE SPOTLIGHT

Not only have Brussels sprouts become the trendiest member of the Brassica family, but they have been pigeonholed for caramelization. No one wants to hear about a Brussels sprout today unless it's roasted, flash fried, or sautéed in bacon fat...

...sorry, the thought of caramelized Brussels sprouts with salty, sweet, fatty bacon is so mesmerizing, I forgot what I was saying. I may actually have forgotten my name...

But it got me thinking, "How do the other Brussels sprouts feel?" Can I create an equally tempting, saliva-inducing dish with no caramelization whatsoever? Some quick reading on other flavors with a strong affiliation for Brussels sprouts offers clear direction. Strong bleu cheese and sharp mustard pair with shallot and vinegar, all folded into farm-fresh butter. Melting over briefly steamed Brussels sprouts, the dish is as tempting as any caramelized concoction.

Okay, these sprouts may not displace their sugary cousins, but they will certainly earn equal billing.

POMEGRANATE GLAZED PARSNIP & CARROT

Serves 6

Sweet carrots and the earthy, spiced flavors of parsnip receive a bright ruby glaze from bright, tart pomegranate juice and seeds.

Ingredients:

- 1 large parsnip
- 1 large carrot
- 1 tbs olive oil
- 1 tbs butter
- ¼ cup Sherry vinegar
- ¼ cup pomegranate juice
- 1 tbs chopped thyme
- White pepper
- ¼ cup pomegranate seeds

Directions:

- Cut parsnip and carrot into ¼" thick and 2–3" long matchsticks.
- Melt butter with olive oil in a 12" skillet over medium heat.
- Add parsnips and carrots to pan and cook 3–4 minutes until they begin to brown in places.
- Cover and cook until vegetables are just about fork tender, still slightly firm in the center.
- Uncover and add vinegar and pomegranate juice. Season lightly with salt and white pepper.
- Cook, stirring, until liquid reduces to a glaze, coating the carrots and parsnips.
- Season to taste with additional salt, pepper and vinegar.
- Serve topped with pomegranate seeds.

SEEDING A POMEGRANATE

Sometime this year you're going to have a bad day at work. You'll come home ready to bark at the dog or lose it with your spouse over something as significant as not changing the toilet paper (I know, it's really annoying!). In the interest of domestic harmony, head to the kitchen and grab a pomegranate. Cut it in half. Hold one half, cut side down, inside a large bowl and begin to beat on the skin with wooden spoon. Soon the seeds will begin to drop saving you the juicy mess and additional frustration of picking them out with your fingers.

I've heard that breaking the pomegranate's insides apart in a bowl of water is even easier. The seeds sink to the bottom as the white pith floats to the top and there is no risk of juice splattering. That, however, sounds less likely to save your marriage. You may want to do it my way.

TIP: To cut carrots into matchsticks, first slice them lengthwise into ¼" thick slabs. Next cut the slabs into ¼" thick strips. Finally, cut the strips down to 2–3" long matchsticks.

KALE SALAD & CAULIFLOWER "GRATIN"

Serves 6–8

Fresh, bitter kale dressed in a sharp vinaigrette is balanced beautifully by creamy cauliflower, rich cheese sauce and crisp, buttery bread crumbs.

For salad:

- ½ pound kale, de-ribbed and cut in ¼" ribbons
- 1 clove garlic, peeled and minced
- ¼ cup red wine vinegar
- ½ cup olive oil—the good stuff!
- 1 tbs grainy mustard

For gratin:

- 4 cups cauliflower florets
- 2 tbs butter
- 1 cup panko bread crumbs
- 1 tbs each chopped thyme and parsley
- 2 cups of the Best Cheese Sauce Ever!

Directions:

Note: Prepare The Best Cheese Sauce Ever! before continuing with recipe (Sidebar).

- Make vinaigrette: On your cutting board, sprinkle garlic with coarse salt and mash into a paste using the flat side of your knife. In a small bowl, whisk together with vinegar, mustard and a grind or three of pepper. While whisking, drizzle oil into vinegar mixture to form a creamy emulsion.
- Toss with kale and let rest for 10 minutes to soften.
- While kale rests, steam cauliflower until tender but still firm.
- Melt butter in small skillet. Toss in breadcrumbs and herbs. Cook until breadcrumbs are golden brown and remove immediately from pan.
- Season cauliflower with salt and pepper, place over kale salad and top with cheese sauce and bread crumbs.

TIP: I find the experience of eating raw kale salads similar to chewing on grass clippings from the front yard. Dressing the kale at least ten minutes before serving makes it tender. Twenty minutes would be even better.

THE BEST CHEESE SAUCE EVER!

Makes about 2 cups

Ingredients:

- 3 tbs unsalted butter
- 3 tbs flour
- 2 cups whole milk
- Nutmeg
- White pepper
- 1 cup shredded cheddar cheese
- ½ cup shredded Gruyère cheese
- 2 tbs dry Sherry
- Cayenne pepper

Directions:

- Melt butter over low heat in a 1 quart saucepan. Stir in flour and cook for 2–3 minutes, being careful not to let brown.
- Pour in milk, whisking briskly to avoid lumps.
- Cook an additional 15–20 minutes, stirring often, until thickened.
- Season to taste with nutmeg and white pepper. Stir in cheese until smooth. Add dry Sherry.
- Season to taste with cayenne, salt and pepper and additional Sherry.

FOXHOLE CONVERSION

Lean in close, I have a confession to make. I don't really care for mashed potatoes. I could take 'em or leave 'em. I know they are prized at dinner tables across this great country, beloved by most, but they just didn't get me excited. Until now.

See, I married into a family from Ohio. In addition to learning the correct response when strangers on the street shouted "O-H" when I wore my T-shirt on game days in the fall, I was told my lukewarm attitude towards mashed potatoes would have to change, and fast.

I decided right then and there that if I was going to have to fall in love with mashed potatoes, I would come up with a recipe so good it would send me back to the table for seconds.

What's the secret to the world's best mashed potatoes? I discovered three things.

1. Use a good starchy potato. Yukon Golds work well for many things, but just won't cut it for mashed. Russets are great, but farmers at my local market introduced me to some newer potatoes like Salem, Eva, Reba and Kennebec, that are flavorful and fantastic. (Really, potatoes do have flavor!)

2. Pass the potatoes through a ricer or food mill*. The less you work them, the fluffier they are. That old fashioned masher makes them lumpy and beaters just make them gummy.

3. Crème fraîche. The one thing lacking amidst the overwhelming comfort of starchy potatoes, rich cream and butter, salt and pepper, was a little bite, something to keep your palate from being lulled to sleep. Crème fraîche— sour cream for grownups—is the perfect answer.

So this year I will finally join those of you who have been extolling their virtues and raise a glass—and a ladle or two of gravy—to a bowl filled with fluffy, rich mashed potatoes. Happy Thanksgiving!

*Bonus! The food mill will catch the skins. No more potato peeling. Don't worry, you can find another job for cousin Johnny!

PERFECT MASHED POTATOES

Serves 6–8

Light and fluffy, rich with just the right bite, these are truly perfect mashed potatoes. There are three keys to this recipe: starchy Russet potatoes, the food mill or ricer, and the bright tang from crème fraîche.

Ingredients:

    4 large starchy potatoes like Russet, Salem or Eva
    2 tbs butter
    ½ cup cream
    3 tbs crème fraîche

Directions:

- Boil potatoes whole and unpeeled until a paring knife easily pierces to the center.

- Place potatoes, peels and all, in a food mill.

- Using the finest disc, press potatoes through a food mill into a medium bowl.

- Stir butter, cream and crème fraîche into warm potatoes.

- Season to taste with salt, pepper and more crème fraîche if you need a little more bite.

TIP: The potatoes have to be processed while still hot. If you let them cool your potatoes will be gummy and lumpy. If you have to make them ahead of time, finish preparation completely and reheat them.

NEW POTATOES

You might not think much about new potatoes. After all, with the exception of the Yukon Gold craze starting in the late 1980's, a potato is a potato is a potato, right? Not exactly.

Potato farming is driven by two forces. First they are the fourth largest crop measured by world wide production and the largest non-grain. That's a lot of potatoes and a lot of dollars. Secondly, potatoes are a little persnickety about where they are grown, so Pacific Northwest and Idaho potatoes aren't always successful in Maine and New York.

These two factors lead to new potatoes being bred all the time, so keep an eye out and try some. Who knew, with exciting vegetables like Fairytale eggplant and purple carrots, that your next big kitchen adventure could be a potato?

EVERY DAY IN EVERY SEASON.

Growing up, we ate dinner together every night at the table. No matter how busy we were, we would stop and gather for a meal that was cooked fresh by my Mom. It's where we as a family would stay connected and share the events of our days, good and bad.

Today, home-cooked dinners bring my husband Jason and I together. We often share our table with friends and the door is always open, and a place set, for anyone traveling through town—especially family.

Over time, I've learned what my Mom already knew those many years ago. Cooking and sharing good food brings people to the table. By gathering there, we grow and nurture the relationships that matter most—lovers and parents, children and dear friends—and it's where we build new ones, too.

But Mom (who must have been pretty tired at the end of some of those

days) knew something else as well. If good food is what brings people together at the table, then it is those same people who bring us, as cooks, into the kitchen. When we cook—more than sustenance, necessity or thrift—we cook for others. We cook for joy and for love.

At the end of each day (beets and humor aside) it is Jason, my strength, my joy, and the love of my life, who brings me into the kitchen. He is why I cook, and he is who I want to share each and every meal with.

When I visit my parents in Massachusetts, or when cousins drop in for a night at our home in DC, we all hang in the kitchen cooking for a couple of hours with no urgency—because what is happening right then and there between us is so much more important than the time on the clock.

On the worst day, in the longest week, no matter how tired, sick or worried I may be, when that first person steps up to one of my demonstrations, a smile always crosses my face. Flooded with energy and joy, I cook, smile and share for the next several hours without noticing a single minute pass.

That is why I wrote this book. Because I wanted to come into your kitchen. Thank you for inviting me. In a kitchen full of food fresh from the farm and garden, and inspired by everyone who gathers at your table to share and to eat, may you find joy every single day, in every season.

COMMUNITY

NOTHING GREAT IS DONE ALONE.
Thank you to the team that created this book:

To my editor Nancy Mendrala and photographer Matt Hocking for your talents and countless hours; to Peter Gloege who put this work to paper; to Bob Morris of Story Farm who printed it and to Sally Ekus who brought us together; and to Matt Lawrence for making sure everyone (and I mean everyone) knows about it.

To the photographers who captured what I could not say with words—the joy, community, love and utter deliciousness created when we cook and share food: Martha FitzSimon, Jenny Lehman, Megan Peper at MC Photography, and Garry Grueber of Cultivaris.

To those who shared their stories, especially Ellen Wells and Tom and Barbara Mendrala.

To David Schneider and Sean Simmons at 202 Films who share my cooking and my story so beautifully through video.

To those whose sharp and experienced eyes read this book to correct mistakes and protect a voice that felt true: Sue Baysinger, Jonnie Garstka, Kelly Harrison, Mike, Sarah and Laura Jasinski, and Sally Benson.

These recipes were cooked with and inspired by beautiful farm-fresh seasonal food from the following:

From my second home at Washington, DC's historic Eastern Market: Dan Donahue at Agora Farms; Marvin and Josh Ogburn at Long Meadow Farms; Emilio and Carlos Canales at Canales Quality Meats; David and Valerie Fowler at Sunny Side Farm; Noah and Tim at Ashton Farms and Tony—you're on the cover! Thanks to Wave, Mark and Mark at Gardener's Gourmet; Mel Inman Sr and Mel Jr at Market Poultry; José and Consuelo Canales at Canales Deli; and Jorge Canales at Market Grocery. And thanks to Barry Margeson and Katrina Cuffey.

To those from the Eastern Market community: Genevieve and Conan O'Sullivan at Sona Creamery and Renee Shields-Farr at Sapore Oil and Vinegar. And to Leah Daniels at Hill's Kitchen for the things we don't eat—beautiful bowls and durable cookware.

To Ben Walters at Spices, Ltd. in Columbus, Ohio's North Market: I will hop on a plane just to shop with you.

For their wise, generous and gentle council: Joe Judge of Clear Possibilities, Alec Bardzik, Paul Underwood, Colin McLetchie at Five Ways Forward. And for equally generous and steady counsel, Peter Glazer and Steve Littlewood.

To those who offered support and care when I needed it most: for family, the Bardziks, the Forgiels and the Radlingers, to Ali Bennett, Sandy Larsen, Jonathan Schenck and David Blau, Seth Semons, Evan Ribero and to the incredibly understanding Andrew Lightman. To Eric Wahl: I cannot imagine a better partner in the kitchen.

To everyone who gave their time and financial resources to turn this dream into a reality, especially those who contributed to the Kickstarter campaign for this book, I am truly humbled.

There are so many others who have been invaluable in the creation of this book. Please know that you are appreciated.

Finally, my sincere thanks to everyone who has attended one of my live demos, and commented or shared a recipe suggestion through my online community. Please know that I do this—with great joy—for you.

CELEBRATIONS

SEASONS TO TASTE celebrates people coming together, sharing their days, their joy and their lives. Five hosts in particular helped us share that message by opening their homes and supporting this book financially. It would not be in your hands without them.

RICK BISHOP & JOE PATRICK

I thought I felt humble asking my friends Rick and Joe if they would open their home and host a party for the spring section of the book, but it was nothing compared to how I felt when they responded, "We'd be honored. Thank you for asking us." The house was spotless (thanks Joe!) and the gardens beautifully planted for the season. They brought together a group of friends who shared their joy so generously with me and with the camera.

MOM & DAD

My Mom's family, the Forgiels, gather often—for holidays, birthdays and weddings—and for the sheer joy of each other's company. In January, they gathered at my family's home in Western, Massachusetts to laugh, eat and share the day together. I have a proud heritage in my family, both the Bardziks and the Forgiels. It is one of generosity, care and hard work. For that, and for them letting me capture this special day for my cookbook, I am truly grateful.

FARMER BILL

When I need to escape Washington, DC I drive to Doepkens Farm in Gambrills, Maryland. My friend Bill raises cattle, laying hens and field after field of colorful flowers for cutting on a 351 year-old farm his grandfather began working 93 years ago. Each year he generously opens his home on the summer solstice for a fund-raising dinner for the City Choir of Washington. For three years, I've had the pleasure of cooking with produce and meat fresh from the farm. My sincere thanks to Bill and his guests for letting me have the event photographed for this book.

ED & GAIL OVERDEVEST

Ed and Gail own a wonderful nursery in southern New Jersey. Beginning in 2014, I had the pleasure of working with them on a line of naturally grown and sustainably packaged herb and vegetable plants for garden centers. They brought me in to share the message of how—from garden center to garden and home—growing and cooking with fresh ingredients can bring joy to gardeners of all generations. I hope this book does their vision proud.

JASON

My husband Jason shares his home—our home—with a lot of people for both pleasure and business. The two came together ten days before Thanksgiving 2014 when we invited old friends for "Fakesgiving"—a full dinner and celebration, photographer included. With all of our lives busy with work, travel and family, it was a wonderful moment to stop, relax and share time. Thank you Jason for sharing our home so generously.

JONATHAN BARDZIK

THE TEAM

SEASONS TO TASTE is the story of farm-fresh, seasonal ingredients and the people—friends, family and farmers—that cooking and sharing food brings together. Just as it gathers people who bring us joy into the kitchen and around the table, it has brought so many exceptional people into my home, my kitchen and around my dining table, which, appropriately, has served as the workspace for creating much of this book.

While my team develops recipes every week, throughout the year, it was still a herculean effort to pull together four years of recipes, learning and the stories from my live cooking events in only four and a half months. These are the exceptional people who have made this cookbook possible and a true joy.

NANCY MENDRALA

My Director of Operations and Baking and I were clearly fated to work together. We grew up 20 miles apart, in homes with shared Polish immigrant traditions, with parents, her Mother and my Father, who were a year apart at the same highschool—but never knew each other.

In addition to managing the daily operations of a rapidly growing business, Nancy edited this book. As a fellow cook, she reads each recipe and each story not just for grammar and typos, but to see if the quantities and directions make sense, the ingredients and tools easily available to fellow home cooks.

More amazingly, she knows my "voice" almost as well as I do, hearing commas and dashes as the pauses I make when speaking. Thanks to Nancy this book isn't just correct, it is right.

MATT HOCKING

Looking for a photographer to capture our weekly recipe development, I was introduced to Matt by a mutual friend. I admit to being doubtful that anyone would agree to join us, week after week, to photograph food rewarded only by the chance to take pictures and get a fresh, home-cooked meal. But Matt showed up that first week, and every one since, with his camera, a growing passion and an incredible talent (and an appetite!).

A little credit may go to his daily surroundings at work with National Geographic, as a successful IT Project Manager. However it is Matt's understanding of our work in the kitchen—celebrating not just the ingredients but the people who enjoy them—that brings life and joy to his photography. From the beginning he has understood that this work is about sharing a life well lived, not just a collection of recipes.

MARTHA FITZSIMON

I had the pleasure of working with Martha a decade ago in another career. Wanting to capture the joy as farm-fresh food and cooking brought people together, I reached out to her again. Most of the event photos you see in this book from Thanksgiving at our home to the spring party in our friends' backyard and dinner on Bill's farm display joy and friendship seen through her expert eye.

PETER GLOEGE

There is another voice, a silent voice, in this book, but one that speaks clearly from the front cover to the back. Peter designed this book. He laid out every recipe, and chose and cropped each photo—another writer, a true collaborator in telling this story. His voice is both gentle and precise. He brought beautiful life to my first book, *Simple Summer*, and I look forward to working with him on the next.

There are so many others—photographer Megan Peper of MC Photography who captured a winter day with my family in Western, MA. Sue Baysinger, Jonnie Garstka and Kelly Harrison who read the book honing its voice—and finding those last few mistakes. The final read was done by my husband Jason, as always my partner and trusted advisor. To everyone who touched this book with their gifts, thank you.

JONATHAN BARDZIK

JONATHAN BARDZIK

www.jonathanbardzik.com

JONATHAN BARDZIK is a cook, author and storyteller based in Washington, DC. Self-trained with more than 20 years in his home kitchen, Jonathan is inspired by the seasonal, local ingredients he grew up with and finds today at the farm market. Jonathan's culinary passion is to explore those farm and garden-fresh flavors, create food for friends and family, and share his adventures to help others find joy in their own home kitchens.

Jonathan's professional culinary career began in 2011 when he started offering weekly cooking demonstrations at DC's historic Eastern Market. Since then, Jonathan has made more than 150 live appearance at Eastern Market and in venues across the country, including the U.S. Department of Agriculture and the National Geographic Museum. He has developed more than 600 recipes, and has appeared in several video series. His first book, *Simple Summer: A Recipe for Cooking and Entertaining with Ease*, was published in Fall 2013. He is excited to share his next book, *Seasons to Taste*, with you.

Jonathan's background in and long love for horticulture has led to partnerships that highlight the connection between gardening and cooking. Jonathan serves as the culinary face of Footprints, a line of naturally grown and sustainably packaged herb, vegetable and fruiting plants available at garden centers throughout the East Coast. He has partnered with the National Garden Bureau to promote their "Year of the" vegetable program and filmed a video series featuring All-America Selections award-winning varieties of vegetables and herbs, in collaboration with the D.C.-area's Arcadia Farms.

Jonathan's work has caught the attention of local media outlets including DC's WTOP, The Hill Rag and DCist, and garnered national coverage from USA Today, Food Network Magazine, and Thrillist. He was recently recognized by the Farmers Market Coalition as a "Farm Market Hero."

Jonathan's popular website (jonathanbardzik.com) features more than 200 recipes and a collection of videos. He maintains an active community on Facebook, Twitter and Instagram to share and find inspiration for his culinary adventures.

Jonathan is excited to share with you the recipes and stories—and joy—he has cultivated over the past 20 years.